Gardening Techniques

Gardening Techniques

All the skills you need for a successful garden

PUBLISHED BY
THE READER'S DIGEST ASSOCIATION LIMITED
LONDON ■ NEW YORK ■ SYDNEY ■ MONTREAL

Contents

Know your garden

Designing your garden

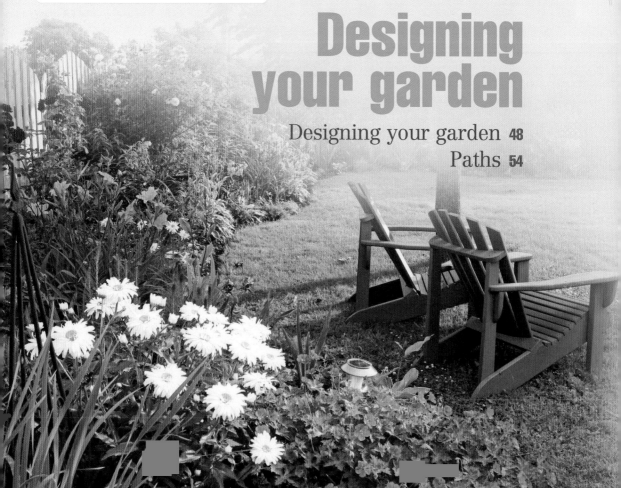

Techniques for plants

Introduction

WHETHER YOU HAVE A SERIES OF POTS ON A BALCONY, a small patio, a modest suburban patch or a large garden with a lot more scope, if you know the right techniques to use, the time you spend gardening will be more successful and more enjoyable and your plants will grow better and last longer. Though some gardening techniques, such as digging, may seem obvious, learning how to do them properly will save time, benefit your garden and save your back.

Understanding your own needs and interest and your plot's site and aspect are the first step. Learn how to work with your local climate, be it dry, windy, prone to frost or flooding. Plan a garden for the time you have available and the way you will use it and choose plants that will thrive in the conditions with minimal maintenance and intervention.

Then start from the bottom up – with your tools and your soil. Select the tools you will need for the kind of garden that you want to create. Discover how to identify the type of soil, the best ways to improve its fertility and the most suitable digging methods to use. Find out how to make compost, how to select fertilisers and manures and how to apply them.

Once the soil is in good condition, we show you how to select suitable plants and how to plant them. Whether you are sowing from seed, or planting ready grown purchased plants, the right planting technique will maximise their chances of a long and healthy life. Just a little more time and skill are needed to propagate your own plants; the book gives a range of both simple and more complex techniques. Learn too, the secret of effective pruning, a technique that helps to control and shape your plants – do it at the right time and in the right way and your plants will thank you for it.

If you love the feel of grass underfoot, find out how to create a luxuriant lawn from turf or from a seed mixture and how to maintain it. Ensure your lawn and plants get the water that they need by installing efficient systems and keep your beds and lawns free from weeds. And if you are interested in growing your own fruit or vegetables, the book suggests ways that you can have a productive plot in even the smallest space.

You probably know what sort of garden you want to have. This book will give you the essential skills you need to create it.

Know your garden

YOUR GARDEN IS AS MUCH A PART OF YOUR HOME AS THE REST OF YOUR PROPERTY. GETTING TO KNOW IT WILL HELP YOU TO ENJOY ALL IT CAN OFFER YOU. WHETHER YOU HAVE LIVED WITH IT FOR SEVERAL YEARS, OR HAVE JUST MOVED IN, A FEW MOMENTS TAKEN TO CONSIDER WHAT IS OUTSIDE THE DOOR WILL SOON PAY DIVIDENDS.

Before doing any work on a garden, you should always consider how much time you have available to tend it; are you a budding enthusiast or someone who's only prepared to spend a couple of hours a week keeping it tidy? What do you use it for? Do you entertain a lot and enjoy having parties outside in summer? Do you have children who need plenty of space to run around and play ball games in, or pets which may dig up new planting or grub up the lawn? Do you like a formal look or something more casual and natural. How much space do you have available and how do you want to use it? All of these should be borne in mind when deciding how to proceed with an existing garden, be it simple maintenance, major new planting; or the creation of a brand new garden.

Paths

A path should be smooth, level or gently sloping, wide enough for two people to pass each other comfortably, without unnecessary sharp curves or bends, and of a material suitable for the purpose for which it is intended. Above all, any path must be safe for all who use it, so potholes, uneven bricks or slabs, slippery wood and algal growth are definitely out.

The outdoor living area

This is where you may want to relax, barbeque or entertain. It is customary for it to be positioned next to the house, but there may be reasons, for example, if this part of the garden is in full shade, or is overlooked, where it might be more satisfactory to place it in another part. It should be big enough for all the activities you enjoy, level and predominantly smooth to accommodate garden furniture.

Walls, fences and hedges

A hedge is generally planted along a boundary or to divide up the plot. Care should be taken to choose the right subjects – if you want privacy, a taller species such as beech or laurel should be used, but it is better to avoid those, like x *cupressocyparis leylandii*, that establish quickly but soon get out of hand. There are many small and slower-growing shrubs that make an ideal hedge. Once mature a hedge will need some regular maintenance such as feeding and clipping or trimming, but is excellent for attracting birds into the garden.

A fence can do a similar job. It is less labour-intensive than a hedge and easier to erect than a wall, but a wooden one has a finite life. On the other hand, there is a wide choice of designs and colours available. It can make a good support for climbing and trained shrubs, but it needs to be accessed periodically for maintenance.

A wall can look magnificent, but the materials may be costly and a certain amount of skill is required in its construction. Furthermore, there may be local authority planning issues. It is important for it to fit in aesthetically with the house, so it is essential to choose the right materials. A wall will provide a sound and permanent support for climbing plants and, like a hedge, can do a lot to block out traffic noise.

The lawn

This helps to show off other features advantageously, and may act as an overspill for the outdoor living area. It can be time and energy consuming as it must be mowed and fed regularly in summer, but many gardeners now prefer not to use moss and weed killers for environmental reasons.

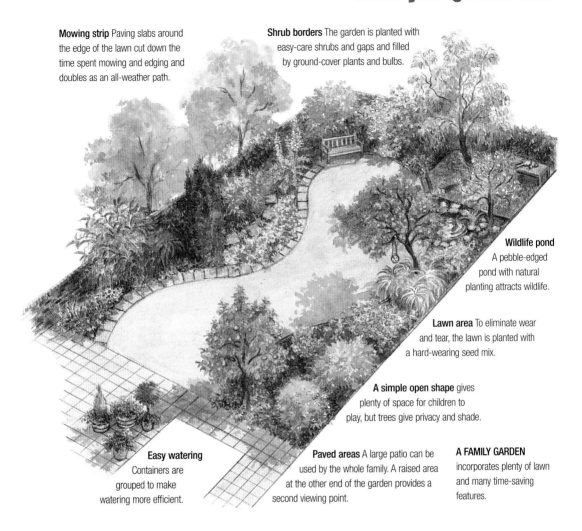

Mowing strip Paving slabs around the edge of the lawn cut down the time spent mowing and edging and doubles as an all-weather path.

Shrub borders The garden is planted with easy-care shrubs and gaps and filled by ground-cover plants and bulbs.

Wildlife pond A pebble-edged pond with natural planting attracts wildlife.

Lawn area To eliminate wear and tear, the lawn is planted with a hard-wearing seed mix.

A simple open shape gives plenty of space for children to play, but trees give privacy and shade.

Easy watering Containers are grouped to make watering more efficient.

Paved areas A large patio can be used by the whole family. A raised area at the other end of the garden provides a second viewing point.

A FAMILY GARDEN incorporates plenty of lawn and many time-saving features.

Beds and borders

Plants are generally more attractive when grouped together in a bed or border. The terms 'bed' and 'border' are often used synonymously to refer to a piece of ground used for growing plants, but technically a bed is surrounded by lawn, paving or similar and is viewed from all sides, while a border is mainly viewed from the front and, to a lesser extent, the sides. It used to be the case that different types of plants were given areas to themselves; for example, a rose bed, shrubbery, herbaceous border, formal bed of annuals, and so on. Nowadays this kind of specialisation can be impractical and most modern gardens will mix all types of plants, including annuals and bulbs.

Rockery

This is an area of gritty soil, usually, but not always, containing rocks positioned to simulate an alpine area. It is often used to edge a garden or to provide a dividing feature between different parts. The plants which tend to be grown in the rockery are generally referred to as alpines. These include true alpines, which originated in mountain areas, and also dwarf perennials, heathers and shrubs.

A rock garden needs regular maintenance so that faster growing subjects do not swamp the slower ones, and routine weeding is essential, as once weeds become established, it is sometimes impossible to remove them without starting again.

Trellis clothed in scented climbers increases the sense of privacy.

Window boxes filled with geraniums add colour and help to frame the view from the living-room window.

THIS SOUTH-FACING GARDEN is a hot spot, is ideal for growing Mediterranean-type plants. The soil is a well-drained sandy loam. The owners like to entertain in the garden, and wanted to include scented plants near the patio, and to have plenty of colour throughout summer.

A combination of slabs, brick pavers, gravel and pebbles make an attractive, all-weather surface.

Flowering shrubs such as ceanothus, hebe and Genista aetensis are at their peak in summer.

Trees

Trees are woody plants grown on a single trunk, and are used in a garden either as shelter from the wind, or more commonly, to provide height within a planting scheme. Ornamental trees should be chosen with care as even those described as 'dwarf' or 'slow-growing' may eventually become too big for a small garden, and are likely to cause structural damage if planted too close to the property or services.

Increasingly nurserymen are catering for the very small plot by training plants that are generally considered to be small shrubs, like cytisus (broom), *Euonymus fortunei* and *Hibiscus syriacus*, to grow on a single stem. These are known as 'standard' shrubs and fulfil the purpose of the ornamental tree where space is very tight.

The kitchen garden

This is an area set aside for the cultivation of vegetables, fruit and herbs. It is not as popular now as it used to be, partly because of the time needed to cultivate food crops, but mainly because many gardens simply do not have the room.

But with the help of plant breeders, who are constantly introducing mini-vegetable varieties that can be grown in tiny spaces, and fruit nurserymen who produce dwarf versions of our most popular fruits and new more intensive methods of cultivation, it is still possible for many gardens to be self-supporting to a large extent, with the help of features such as raised beds, pots, tubs, trellises and by adding attractive edible plants to the mixed border, window box and hanging basket.

Greenhouse and cold frame

A greenhouse enables the gardener to raise a wide variety of plants from seed and cuttings, overwinter half-hardy patio plants, grow exotic subjects needing the protection of glass for some or all of the year, and produce early fruit and vegetables. Heating the greenhouse increases the range of activities, but can be costly. Always position the greenhouse in the sunniest spot available. A cold frame is useful for hardening off bedding and half-hardy vegetable plants and for certain types of propagation. If space is restricted, you may find you can manage with just a cold frame, and there ar
vertica ! cold

The compost area

Every garden should have adequate means of composting green kitchen and garden waste, including leaves, weeds, vegetable peelings and waste crops, and there are many efficient compost bins on the market. Many local authorities now encourage home composting by providing free or heavily subsidised bins. Two bins are better than one, as one can finish rotting while you are filling the other.

The conventional place for the compost bin is in the vegetable garden. However, without a vegetable garden the most convenient site is a sunny spot near the ell-made compost is l should not attract flies.

IN AN AWKWARD,
devices have been
depth, while keepir

sely planted to screen
l to suppress weeds.

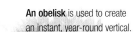

An obelisk is used to create an instant, year-round vertical.

ngle to make the garden look bigger than it really is. The angle is softened by curving it.

Stepping-stones are recessed to lie flush with the lawn, so the lawnmower can pass straight over them.

CLIMATE AND WEATHER ARE THE TWO ISSUES THAT HAVE THE MOST INFLUENCE ON HOW YOUR GARDEN GROWS. THEY VARY GREATLY ACCORDING TO WHAT PART OF THE COUNTRY YOU LIVE IN, BUT THERE ARE ALSO LOCAL CONDITIONS THAT CAN CAUSE DIFFERENCES, EVEN IN THE SAME IMMEDIATE LOCALITY.

The growing season

The period when plants are in active growth is called the growing season. The length of the season depends mainly on soil temperature, beginning when it reaches about 7°C and ending when it drops below this figure, but the length of the days also has some influence.

Regional variation

The extreme south west of England – Cornwall and southern parts of Devon – has the longest growing season, which can be up to 360 days a year, while the Scottish Highlands have the shortest – as few as 150 days in colder years. The average for the rest of the United Kingdom is 250 days.

Higher average temperatures in the past few years have meant that the growing season has lengthened by several days in many parts of the country and plants are sprouting and flowering considerably earlier.

Climate

General climate

This is affected by four main factors – altitude, latitude, prevailing wind and proximity to the sea. Gardens in the south of the country are warmer, and therefore have a longer growing season, than those further north; those high in the Pennine Hills are much colder than those at lower altitudes but with the same latitude. Coastal gardens in the west have a near sub-tropical climate because of the Gulf Stream, but in general all coastal gardens have a more equable climate because the sea prevents temperature peaks and troughs.

Local climate

This is affected by the slope of the garden, shade, soil type, shelter or lack of it and closeness to large areas of water. A garden on a south-facing slope has a longer growing

Draw up a plan of your garden and mark areas that are in the sun and shade during the day. Use different kinds of hatching to show the different levels of shade and highlighter pens to show roughly the amount of sunlight in different parts of the garden. Indicate any problem areas such as wet or dry spots.

On an exposed site such as a coastal garden, wind can cause more damage than frost and cold. The first step in such a location is to provide some shelter. Filter the wind to slow it down with a hedge or an artificial windbreak, which will give useful shelter for a distance of about ten times its height to the leeward side. Here, a shelter belt of pines and shrubs protects more decorative salt-resistant plants from the prevailing wind. Planting 'windows' have been left on either side of the eucalyptus to guide the eye to sea views.

season than one on level ground, and particularly one facing north. Clay soil takes longer to warm up than a loamy, peaty or sandy one, but sandy soils can be more subject to frosts. You can help to warm up a cold soil by covering it with fleece, polythene, weed control fabric or cloches for a few weeks before planting if you want to extend the growing season of a particular piece of ground.

An unsheltered plot can be subjected to battering and chilling winds, but shelter may cast shade, creating cooler pockets of ground. A large stretch of water nearby, such as a lake or reservoir, will have a cooling effect on hot days, and may also affect local rainfall. A garden surrounded by high buildings or many tall trees may be in virtually total shade, with consequent reduced temperatures and light.

Microclimate
This is the climate that exists in a small area – a garden, border or even surrounding a single plant. Microclimates are created by many things. Walls, fences, hedges and plants will cast shade and reduce temperature and light; they can also cause a rain shadow and make nearby ground drier than in other parts of the garden. Frost pockets can also occur if cold air is trapped by fences, hedges and other screens, especially at the base of a slope if the chilled air cannot escape to a lower level. However,

screening the garden will also provide shelter from wind and scorching sunshine, and the heat retention of walls and buildings helps to keep the nearby air temperature a degree or two higher. You can create a microclimate if necessary, using temporary or permanent windbreaks, or cloches.

Weather

Rainfall

Average rainfall varies considerably throughout the British Isles, from the driest areas in the east of England to the wettest – the Lake District and the mountains of Scotland and Wales. All garden plants in the United Kingdom require a reasonable amount of rain in order to thrive, but if you live in one of the drier regions, choosing plants tolerant of such conditions will both improve the look of the garden and make life easier by reducing the necessity for regular watering.

The wettest time of the year is usually from October to January, but in recent years rainfall and dry spells have been much harder to predict and periods of drought (a period of 15 or more consecutive days without appreciable rainfall) have been much more common. Snow can be beneficial to plants as it acts as a protective blanket, but this has become much less in most parts of the country during the past few years.

Frost

This occurs when the temperature falls below 0ºC. It is harmful to plants because it freezes sap in the leaves and stems of vulnerable species and ruptures their cell walls. Furthermore, frozen water in the soil cannot be absorbed by the roots so during prolonged frost a plant can die from a shortage of water.

A late spring frost, when new growth has already started, is particularly damaging, so if one is forecast be prepared to cover up with fleece or old net curtains

Coping with dry soil
■ Choose drought-tolerant plants.
■ Conserve moisture by mulching in spring when the soil is moist.
■ Mulch problem soils – too dry, sandy or chalky – twice a year, in spring and autumn.
■ Build a deep, no-dig bed if you want to grow fruit and vegetables.
■ Don't try to grow a conventional grass lawn. Instead, create patches of green with a herb lawn using thyme or camomile.

any plants that might suffer. A frost is predictable from late autumn to early spring when the evening sky is clear and wind is light.

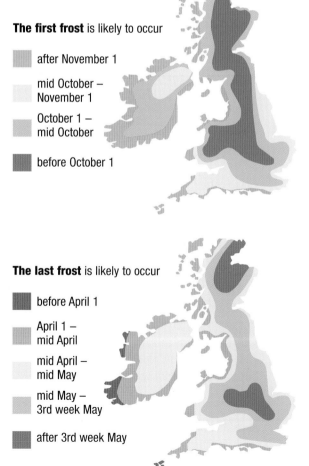

The first frost is likely to occur

■ after November 1

■ mid October – November 1

■ October 1 – mid October

■ before October 1

The last frost is likely to occur

■ before April 1

■ April 1 – mid April

■ mid April – mid May

■ mid May – 3rd week May

■ after 3rd week May

Potentilla (left) and allium (right) will both grow in an exposed, windy site; alliums will thrive in poor soils and tolerate salty spray.

Wind

A light breeze can be beneficial, blowing away old plant material and drying out waterlogged soil, but a gale, from any direction but especially from the north or east that has added wind chill factor, can do tremendous damage, breaking branches, uprooting trees and bushes, and stripping young leaves from plants. A shelterbelt or windbreak that filters the wind will bring enormous benefit, but avoid solid wind breaks, which will create downdraughts on both sides that can flatten a planted border in a very short time, so choose a hedge rather than a wall for wind protection.

Temperature

Many plant functions depend on temperature – dormancy, seed germination, growth, flowering, ripening – sometimes, though not always, connected to day length. Average temperatures are generally higher in the south and west of the country, and lower at higher altitudes. Lately, average temperatures have been one or two degrees higher throughout the year, which has led to earlier springs, more prolific flowering and seed production and later onset of winter, and this change has affected all areas of the UK, enabling many plants to be grown outdoors which previously needed greenhouse protection during part or all of the year. High summer temperatures are not entirely beneficial as flower life is shortened, the soil dries out quickly and the germination of some seeds requiring cooler conditions is impaired. To be successful, a gardener needs to appreciate this, and all other aspects of the prevailing weather in the locality, right from the start.

Solutions for windy spots

■ **Reduced growth** Wind slows plant growth by increasing water loss through evaporation. This can significantly reduce the yields of vegetables so protect the vegetable plot with windbreak netting.

■ **Poor pollination** Pollinating insects avoid windy areas, so to get good pollination of fruit crops grow them against sheltered walls.

■ **Vulnerable plants** Avoid plants with big leaves and those that come into flower early in the season because they are more vulnerable to damage from the wind.

■ **New plants** It is essential to protect new plants, especially evergreens, because they are particularly susceptible to wind damage. Protect them with temporary windbreak netting until well established. Keep all new plants well watered.

Hand tools for gardeners

A FEW BASIC TOOLS WILL ENABLE YOU TO ACCOMPLISH MOST GARDEN TASKS, BUT SOME
EXTRA ITEMS DESIGNED FOR PARTICULAR JOBS WILL ADD VERSATILITY TO YOUR TOOL KIT.
YOU MAY ALSO WANT TO TRY OUT A FEW MORE SPECIALISED ITEMS OF EQUIPMENT, SOME
OF WHICH YOU MAY EVENTUALLY FIND INDISPENSABLE.

Buying tools

Durable, well-made tools are a pleasure
to handle and can make light work of
gardening tasks, so always buy the best you
can afford. Make sure the tool is right for
the job and ask for advice if you are in
doubt. Before buying, test it for comfort,
balance, size and weight; a tool that is too
heavy will be tiring to use over a long period
of time, while a handle that is too short or
long for you can cause wrist or back injury.

Compare the relative merits of the
different materials the tool may be made
from. For example, wooden handles are
more shock-absorbent than metal ones.
Stainless-steel or Teflon-coated blades are
easier to use and to clean, especially if you
garden on sticky clay.

Caring for tools

Tools that are regularly cleaned and
neatly stored are always ready for use.

■ **Allocate storage space** for each tool
where it is easily accessible and cannot be
damaged. Suspend large items with cutting
edges, such as spades and hoes, from hooks
or clips on a wall or door and keep smaller
tools together in a drawer or a box.

■ **Clean all tools after use**. Scrape or brush
off soil and plant debris, especially from the
handles, where hardened soil can cause
discomfort during use. Wipe metal blades
with an oily rag to prevent rust.

■ **Keep cutting tools sharp**. Pruning
equipment needs regular honing to keep it
sharp so that it cuts without damaging the
plant, and without undue effort. Spade and

Essential basic kit

The equipment shown here is described
in detail on the following pages:

■ spade *(see page 19)*
■ fork *(see page 19)*
■ trowel *(see page 21)*
■ secateurs *(see page 21)*
■ lawnmower *(see page 26)*
■ watering can *(see page 25)*
■ pocket knife *(see page 22)*
■ gardening gloves

USEFUL EXTRAS

The following additional tools and
equipment will almost certainly be useful:

■ rake *(see page 19)*
■ hoe *(see page 20)*
■ shears *(see page 22)*
■ hand fork *(see page 21)*
■ hand cultivator *(see page 21)*
■ bucket *(see page 22)*
■ hosepipe *(see page 23)*

Regular use of a sharpening stone will keep blades sharp, making spades and hoes easier to use.

hoe blades are easier to use if you hammer out dents and sometimes file the edge sharp.
▪ **Clean, sharpen and oil or grease** all metal parts.
▪ **At the end of the growing season,** inspect tools before storing them. Clean thoroughly. Check and repair damaged handles, and wipe wooden parts with linseed oil.

Cultivation tools

Several versatile tools are designed for soil preparation, planting and weeding tasks. Stainless-steel models are more expensive but easier to use and to clean.

Spades, forks and rakes

▪ **Spade** Used primarily for digging, making planting holes and moving or mixing soil, a spade is also useful for skimming off weeds, tidying border edges and mixing compost. The blade – of stainless, forged or coated steel – is attached to a wooden or metal shaft fitted with a plastic

or wooden D or T-shaped handle. In a good-quality spade, the blade and tubular neck are forged from a single piece of metal for strength, and the blade has a tread for comfort. Standard spades have a 28 x 20cm blade and a 70cm–1m shaft, but a border spade has a smaller blade for working in small spaces or where a lighter model is easier to use.

▪ **Fork** A garden fork is used for general cultivation work, such as breaking down soil after digging, pricking over and loosening the surface. It can also be used for moving or lifting crops, plants and bulky manure. Most forks have four metal prongs, or tines, forged from a single piece of metal, and are fitted with the same kinds of shafts and handles as spades. On a standard fork, the head or tines are 30 x 20cm long, but a border fork has smaller tines.

TIP Gardeners who find digging and cultivating difficult may find a spade and fork with special cranked handles or a spade with a sprung blade a useful solution.

▪ **Rake** A soil rake is used for levelling and surface preparation, especially when making a seedbed. The long wooden or plastic-covered metal handle is attached to a steel head fitted with forged steel tines. As you move the head backwards and forwards over soil, the tines loosen the surface and break up lumps as you level the ground.

Smaller and lighter than standard tools, a border fork (left) and rake (right) are useful for working in confined spaces or where plants grow tightly together.

Held in a more upright position, a rake can be used to comb stones and weeds across the surface. Once you have prepared a seedbed, you can turn the rake over and use a corner to draw out a drill for sowing.

Hoes

The most important hoes are the dutch, or push, hoe and the draw, or swan-necked, hoe. These can be used for making sowing drills and covering seeds with soil, as well as for weeding. Choose one you can use without bending your back.

■ **Dutch hoe** The flat rectangular blade is attached to a long handle at a slight angle. To loosen soil and destroy weeds, as you walk backwards, push the hoe to and fro, with the blade just below the surface.

■ **Draw hoe** The rectangular or semi-circular head, joined to the handle at a right angle, is used to chop out weeds and break up the surface while moving forwards. It is also good for scraping off stones and earthing up potatoes.

Using a spade or fork
■ Keep your back straight.
■ Insert the full head of the spade or fork vertically into the soil to its maximum depth.
■ When lifting soil or plants, steady the handle with one hand and move the other close to the head.
■ Clean the head regularly during use by plunging it into a bucket of sand or scraping it with a flat piece of wood or a paint scraper.

Other types of hoe

■ **Tined hoe** The curved prongs of this hoe are effective for deeper cultivation as well as for weeding.

■ **Onion hoe** This is a short-handled draw hoe designed for weeding between closely spaced plants.

A dutch hoe is ideal for getting rid of young weeds.

The draw hoe's angled head will chop off weeds as it moves forwards.

A hand trowel is one of the most essential garden tools, particularly for surface cultivation.

Hand tools

■ **Trowel** Used for surface cultivation – planting, removing weeds, loosening the soil surface and marking out seed drills – as well as for measuring small amounts of soil, compost or fertiliser. The rounded, tapering blade, sometimes with cranked neck, is fitted with a 10–15cm wooden or plastic handle. When choosing a trowel, make sure that the head is forged from a single piece of steel and fitted to the handle with a separate ring or ferrule.

■ **Hand fork** Of similar construction and size to a trowel, this has three or four flattened tines and is used for weeding in confined spaces, lifting young plants and lightly cultivating small areas such as pots, window boxes and growing bags.

■ **Hand cultivator** This tined tool is used to loosen and aerate soil between plants and in spaces where a hoe cannot reach.

■ **Bulb planter** Used to bore holes in soil or a lawn when planting bulbs, this can save time when transplanting small pot-grown plants, which often neatly fit the 8cm wide holes, or even planting potatoes. It is a tapering steel cylinder attached to a short or long handle at one end, with cutting teeth at the other.

Buy the best secateurs you can afford; if you have a lot of woody shrubs, anvil types (right) may be a better choice than bypass (left).

Pruning and maintenance

Having the right tools for routine jobs like pruning, watering and tidying will make them seem less of a chore.

Secateurs and loppers

The two main types of secateurs are for use on stems up to 1cm thick. Ratchet types can make cutting easier, as does a rubber stop fitted between the handles. Check that hand grips are comfortable and fit the span of your hand when open. Avoid cheap models, which are suitable only for light work. Left-handed models are available.

■ **Bypass secateurs** Operating with a scissors action, these are used for most kinds of pruning, deadheading and trimming plants to size and shape.

■ **Anvil secateurs** A single sharp blade cuts against a flat surface, making these ideal for cutting hard, woody stems.

■ **Loppers** Long-handled pruners will cut stems up to about 2.5cm in diameter. They

Use a hand cultivator (left) to loosen soil. A bulb planter (right) saves time when planting out bulbs or pot-grown plants.

are fitted with anvil or bypass secateur heads, often with a ratchet to reduce the effort needed to cut hard, thick stems. Test for balance and weight before buying.

■ **Tree loppers or long-arm pruners** The cutting heads are on the end of fixed or extending poles up to 5m long.

Saws

■ **Pruning saw** A fixed or folding pruning saw will cut branches that are thicker than 2.5cm in diameter. The straight or curved handle and blade are designed for easy access in confined places between branches. Unlike wood-working saws, the large toughened teeth will often cut only on the pulling stroke.

■ **Bow saw** A disposable blade is tensioned between the ends of a bent tubular handle. It is used for the largest tree branches.

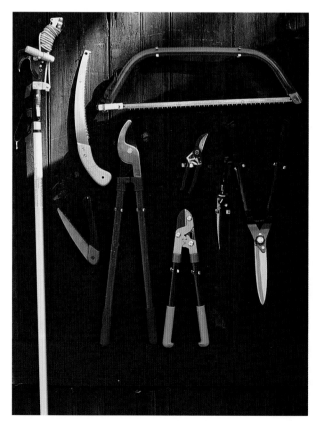

Choose pruning tools according to the needs of your garden: clockwise from left: tree pruners on fixed pole; pruning saw; bow saw; garden shears; one-handed shears; bypass secateurs; anvil loppers; bypass loppers; folding pruning saw.

Shears

■ **Garden shears** Lightweight and heavy-duty models are available for trimming hedges, shrubs and small areas of grass. Straight-edged kinds are easy to sharpen and maintain, while those with wavy cutting edges are effective for cutting thicker stems, but need care with sharpening. Some have long or extending handles for greater reach. Test for weight and balance before buying.

■ **One-handed shears** Sprung to open automatically, these are useful for light trimming, deadheading and for cutting small areas of grass. They may be fitted with swivelling blades to adjust the angle of cut.

Garden knives

■ **Pruning knife** This has a curved, folding blade and is used for trimming off thin sideshoots, cleaning up the edges of pruning wounds and taking cuttings.

■ **Pocket knife** A sharp pocket knife has a multitude of uses, from cutting string and opening bags of fertiliser to trimming and pruning plants. Most models have a blade that folds away.

Carrying equipment

■ **Bucket** Useful for carrying and watering. Plastic buckets are cheaper than metal ones, but have a shorter life.

■ **Carrying sheets and bags** Made of tearproof woven plastic, carrying sheets and bags are useful for tidying the garden and for carrying prunings, trimmings and soft weeds. They are light and easily stored.

■ **Watering can** Buy the largest you can carry when full. For general use, choose a 9 litre model but for the greenhouse choose a lighter 4.5 litre model with a long spout. You need two roses (sprinkler heads): fine for watering

Good-quality carrying equipment will make gardening less tiring. A wheelbarrow and watering can are essential; a bucket, plastic carrying sheet and bags are useful extras.

Lawn-watering equipment

Watering a lawn in dry weather is essential to keep it looking green throughout summer.

Hosepipes

■ **Hosepipe** The best hosepipes are reinforced with nylon, which prevents kinking and increases its life; make sure it will reach to the end of the garden. You need an appropriate connector to attach it to a tap and possibly a spray nozzle for the other end. A wall-mounted reel is convenient for storing and a freestanding reel on wheels for storing and moving the hose around.
■ **Leaky pipe and seep hose** These perforated hosepipes can be laid on a lawn and moved around every so often to deliver a fine spray or a gentle trickle of water. They are less wasteful of water than sprinklers.

Propagation equipment

When sowing seed and taking cuttings, the right compost and equipment, with a few specialised tools, will increase your chances of success.

seeds and seedlings, and coarse for general watering. Make sure it has a large enough opening for easy filling.
■ **Wheelbarrow** Useful for transporting heavy materials such as soil, compost and larger tools. They are usually fitted with a single wheel; for use over long distances, a pneumatic tyre is more comfortable than a solid one. Two-wheeled barrows are more stable on uneven ground. Some models can be fitted with side extensions for carrying leaves, and collapsible models are also available where storage space is limited.
■ **Trug** Useful for carrying garden tools as well as for transporting cut flowers and freshly harvested produce. Treat wooden trugs annually with preservative or linseed oil to keep them in good condition.

Watering can roses are available in a range of different sizes.

Containers

■ **Pots** Stock up with a selection, from 6–8cm for individual seedlings and cuttings to 20–25cm for large plants and greenhouse shrubs. Square pots hold more compost than round ones and pack closer together on the greenhouse staging. Extra-deep pots are for long-rooted seedlings such as sweet peas.

Degradable pots made of peat, coir or paper are ideal for propagating plants that resent root disturbance, as they are planted out with their contents to gradually decompose in the soil.
■ **Trays** Full or half-size trays are usually shallow and made of thin plastic that lasts for only a few seasons. Most can be fitted with a clear lid for germinating seeds and rooting cuttings. Some are divided into cells for

A selection of seed trays, including modular trays and cellular inserts, plastic pots, paper tubes and degradable coir pots (far left).

growing plants separately, or can be fitted with cellular inserts for sowing large seeds or pricking out individual seedlings.

■ **Pans** Like pots but only a third or half as deep, pans are useful for sowing seeds and raising shallow-rooted, slow-growing plants like alpines and dwarf bulbs.

Other items

■ **Rooting hormone** Dip the lower tips of cuttings in this liquid or powdered hormone suspension to aid rooting. Store in a refrigerator and discard after a year.

■ **Copper fungicide** A powdered or liquid concentrate that is diluted, then watered onto seedlings and freshly sown seeds as protection against damping-off and other fungal diseases.

■ **Sieve** A meshed sieve, or riddle, is used to separate coarse compost or soil from finer particles, especially when covering seeds and preparing a seedbed. Buy sieves with different meshes or buy one with a selection of graded inserts. Wire mesh is more durable than plastic.

■ **Knife** A folding pocket or craft knife is essential for cuttings. Keep it dry and very sharp, and sterilise the blade after use.

■ **Dibber** A slim, tapered tool used when transplanting seedlings to make holes in compost. Some have a two-pronged fork at the other end for separating and lifting

A metal compost tidy separates an area of staging for potting up.

A thermometer, plant labels and pocket knife are invaluable for sowing and propagating under glass.

The simplest is a clear plastic-covered box that takes a few seed trays. Electrically heated propagating trays are available for use on windowsills. The most sophisticated type is a large frame for staging, fitted with a hinged lid, soil heating cable and thermostat, and automatic misting unit.

▧ **Glass** Small panes of clear glass are useful for covering pots and trays of seeds to prevent them from drying out.

▧ **Plastic bags** Keep a stock of new or used clear bags to enclose pots and trays of cuttings to keep humidity levels high.

Watering equipment

▧ **Water trays** These are useful for pots and trays that need watering from below. You can buy purpose-made shallow plastic trays or use an old roasting tin.

▧ **Long-spouted watering can** A small watering can with a long spout fitted with a very fine rose is ideal for gently watering seed trays and seedlings and for reaching over the staging.

▧ **Mister** Several 500ml hand sprays will be useful for misting cuttings and young plants. Keep one filled with water and others, labelled, for copper fungicide solution or diluted liquid feed.

▧ **Capillary matting** This reduces the need to water and is useful if you are away for any length of time.

seedlings. Larger models, sheathed with a metal nose, are for planting and transplanting outdoors. Improvise with a pencil under glass and sharpened broken spade handle outdoors.

▧ **Widger** Like a narrow, fluted spatula, it is useful for lifting out seedlings and rooted cuttings without disturbing their neighbours.

▧ **Labels** Use plastic labels and a soft lead pencil to identify seeds and seedlings. Coloured ones are useful for distinguishing between batches of plants. Labels used outdoors must be weather-resistant and conspicuous; use a waterproof marker.

▧ **Thermometers** Temperature levels are important under glass, especially in a propagator, where the right amount of heat is critical for germination. Use a maximum-minimum thermometer to record the daily range of temperatures, and a soil thermometer to test composts, cuttings beds in propagating cases and outdoor seedbeds.

▧ **Propagator** For a controlled environment in which to root cuttings and germinate seedlings, a propagator is almost essential.

Capillary matting absorbs water from a reservoir at the side so plants can take up water as required.

Lawnmowers

The type and size of lawnmower you need will depend on the size of your lawn, your budget and how much effort you want to put into mowing. Mowers are defined by their cutting action and how they are powered.

Cutting action

■ **Cylinder mowers** These have a number of blades arranged in a spiral to form a rotating cylinder. Cutting occurs as the blades pass close to a fixed blade set just below the cylinder, rather like the action of scissor blades. The cut quality depends on the rotation speed of the cylinder, how closely the rotating blades are passing the fixed blade and the number of blades on the cylinder – the more blades, the finer the cut.

■ **Rotary mowers** A single blade or several blades, made from toughened metal or a hardened plastic, rotate horizontally at high speed, slicing through the grass. The effectiveness of the cut depends on the speed of rotation and the blades' sharpness.

Both types of mower produce a good finish if used correctly, but only rotary mowers can cope with cutting down long grass. Both will also produce a striped effect if equipped with a roller behind the cutting blades – stripes result not from the cutting action but from the roller pressing down the grass.

Means of power

The models discussed here are all walk-behind mowers; ride-on mowers are too large for the average garden.

■ **Non-powered cylinder mowers** are driven entirely by human energy. They have a restricted cutting width of 25–45cm and can be tiring to use, especially on a large lawn, but are useful if you have only a small grassed area.

■ **Petrol or diesel-powered mowers** are fitted with a two or four-stroke engine. Models may be cylinder, rotary or rotary hover (which float just above the ground rather than rely on wheels).

■ **Mains electricity-powered mowers** have a heavy-duty electric motor, and cylinder, rotary and rotary hover types are all available. They are light to use, but there must be a handy power socket and the working area is restricted by the length of cable. It is important to follow a cutting pattern to avoid accidental damage to the cable; always use a residual circuit breaker (RCB) in case of accidents.

■ **Battery-operated cylinder mowers** incorporate a motor and a heavy-duty battery, with a charger. The weight of the battery tends to make this type of mower heavier than others.

Mains electricity-powered cylinder mowers are available in a wide range of sizes, suitable for tiny lawns and much larger areas.

A strimmer (left) is useful for neatening small spaces. Leaf blowers (right) may blow leaves into neat piles or suck them into a bag.

Other cutting tools

A number of other implements are available for specific trimming jobs around lawn edges and for awkward places where lawnmowers cannot be used.

▓ **Strimmers** Light, hand-held machines that are useful for trimming long grass around trees or in difficult corners. Powered by a two-stroke petrol engine or mains electricity, they cut using a length of nylon cord rotating horizontally at high speed.

▓ **Leaf blower or vacuum** A hand-held machine with a strong fan powered by a two-stroke petrol engine or mains electricity. It blows leaves and debris into one area or sucks them into a chamber or bag. A push-along leaf sweeper collects leaves, debris and dead grass but is not effective when leaves and grass are wet.

Sprinklers

Attached to the end of a hosepipe, a sprinkler is convenient for watering a large area of grass.

▓ **Static sprinklers** spray a circular area of the lawn.

▓ **Oscillating sprinklers** revolve or swing from side to side and cover a wide area; the reach is adjustable.

▓ **Travelling sprinklers** creep slowly across the lawn, powered by the water flow.

▓ **'Pop up' sprinklers** are permanently installed below lawns and rock gardens; they remain out of sight until water pressure pushes them above ground.

Cultivating a large area

Petrol-powered rotavators or cultivators are excellent for tilling a larger garden, turning in weeds and mixing in manure or compost. Attachments are available for earthing up, making seedbeds and tilling between crops. Most machines can be set to work at different depths and some have adjustable handles, allowing you to walk to one side on uncultivated soil. Buy a sturdy, easily managed model, suited to the size of the garden, and maintain it regularly, or hire an appropriate type and cultivate as much ground as possible in one go.

Powered hedge-trimmers

An electric or petrol-powered hedge-trimmer can save time and effort if you have a large hedge and can be hired. With either single or double-sided reciprocating blades, these powerful machines require great care during use. Always keep power cables safely out of the way, and use a circuit breaker. Wear thick gloves, goggles and ear defenders.

An oscillating sprinkler can be wasteful of water so avoid if you live in an area prone to shortages. But it is useful for covering a large area of the garden.

28 What kind of soil?

SOIL IS THE RAW MATERIAL OF A GARDEN, MADE UP OF FOUR BASIC COMPONENTS: SAND, SILT, CLAY AND ORGANIC MATERIAL. THE VARYING PROPORTIONS OF THESE WILL DETERMINE SOIL TEXTURE AND HOW WELL PLANTS GROW.

Soil type and texture

You need to know what type of soil you are dealing with and its pH value (acidity/alkalinity), as this will influence how you cultivate the soil and the time of year you do it. Heavy clay soils are best cultivated in autumn before they become too wet, and sandy soils in late winter and spring. The pH will to an extent dictate the plants you can grow – you should avoid trying to grow acid-loving plants on chalk soil, for example. You can test the pH using a kit; it is a good idea to take samples from different areas of the garden.

Sandy soils are at least 70 per cent sand and gravel and no more than 15 per cent clay. The colour varies, depending on their organic matter content. They are very free-draining and often lack fertility, but do have the advantage of warming up quickly in spring. They feel gritty when rubbed between finger and thumb.

Clay soils contain at least 45 per cent clay, and less than 40 per cent sand. Their high water-holding capacity means they drain slowly; some are prone to waterlogging. Most are quite fertile and good at holding plant nutrients, but they can be difficult to cultivate and are often slow to warm up in spring. They have a smooth, soap-like texture when moistened and rubbed between finger and thumb.

Chalky soils have a high concentration of chalk or limestone (it may be visible as pieces of rock) and are often shallow, with soil depth less than 30cm over the rock below. They can be very fertile and are usually biologically active, with high populations of worms and beneficial bacteria. They tend to be free-draining, but high pH limits the range of plants they can support.

Peaty soils are correctly termed 'organic' as a relatively high level of organic matter (minimum 15 per cent) influences their characteristics. They are good at retaining water and can be very fertile (unless they are pure peat). Although this type of soil is usually associated with plants that love acid conditions, there are many alkaline organic soils. They feel loose, crumbly and fibrous when handled.

Silty soils are often referred to as loams. They contain at least 70 per cent silt with a clay content that is below 12 per cent. Many gardeners view these as ideal soils. This is because they are usually good at holding water and are also free-draining, fertile, productive and easier to work than most other types of soil. They feel smooth but slightly gritty when they are moistened and rubbed between the finger and thumb.

Understanding pH values

Whether soil is acid, alkaline or neutral will determine the range of plants that can be grown in it. Acidity and alkalinity are measured using the pH scale, which ranges from 0–14; pH 7 is neutral, neither acid nor alkaline (see below).

Most natural soils range from pH 4 to pH 9; few plants will grow in soil that has a pH above 9 or below 4. Gardeners should usually aim at a soil with a pH of 6.5–7 to ensure they are able to grow the maximum range of plants.

TESTING TIP You should always avoid handling soil samples with your bare hands when testing the pH, as the pH of your skin may affect the final reading.

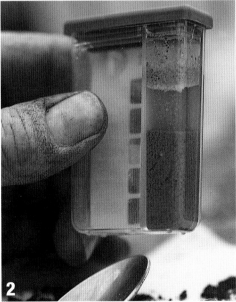

Soil testing

1 Following the instructions with the kit, use an old spoon or a trowel to dig up a sample of moist soil from the top 15cm and place it on a sheet of absorbent paper. With the back of the trowel or spoon, crush the sample lightly to break down lumps, and remove and discard any stones or roots. Put a measured amount of soil into the test tube with a measured amount of test chemical, and add distilled water to the level indicated on the tube. Seal the top and shake the contents vigorously for about a minute, then allow the solution in the tube to settle and clear.

2 The liquid will gradually change colour as it settles. Check its final colour against the pH indicator card to get a reasonably accurate reading of the lime content in the soil. The two samples tested below show a range of soils from the acid end of neutral to alkaline.

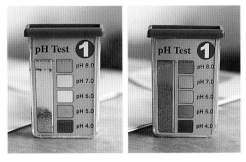

pH Test ❶ pH 8.0 / pH 7.0 / pH 6.0 / pH 5.0 / pH 4.0

pH Test ❶ pH 8.0 / pH 7.0 / pH 6.0 / pH 5.0 / pH 4.0

pH scale

0	1	2	3	4	5	6	7	8	9	10	11	12	13	14
		ACID						NEUTRAL					ALKALINE	

DIGGING OVER VACANT GROUND WITHIN FLOWER BORDERS AND VEGETABLE PLOTS AT LEAST ONCE EACH YEAR IS A GOOD WAY OF INCORPORATING ORGANIC MATTER INTO THE SOIL, IMPROVING DRAINAGE AND ROOT PENETRATION.

Digging is the most effective way of preparing the soil for the next growing season and also keeps the garden tidy by burying unwanted plant waste and weeds. But especially when soil is being brought back into cultivation from a neglected state, disturbing the soil in this way will lead to the emergence of weeds, as most of their dormant seeds will start to germinate once exposed to daylight.

If you have a bed of shallow-rooted plants, it may not be necessary to dig to a greater depth than about 30cm. Exceptions are if the soil has become compacted or is heavy and badly drained.

Single digging

The most commonly practised form of digging cultivates the soil to the depth of a spade blade (called a spit), usually about 25–30cm deep. Cultivation is concentrated in the area where most plant roots naturally grow, in the top 10–20cm of soil.

If the plot is large, mark out the area to be dug using canes and a garden line, then dig a trench at one end (see below). A new trench is created each time a section of the plot is dug. Repeat this process until the entire plot has been dug. Keep your back as straight as possible when lifting spadefuls of soil to avoid strain and injury.

Single digging

YOU WILL NEED:
- garden line and canes to mark out plot (optional)
- spade
- fork to loosen soil
- wheelbarrow

1 Dig the first trench to one spade width and one spade depth.
2 Place the soil from this trench in a wheelbarrow and take it to the far end of the plot – or place it in a corner of the plot. It will be used later to fill in the final trench.

Double digging

This technique is often used where a hard sub-surface layer of soil has formed, or on land that is being cultivated for the first time. It involves digging to the equivalent depth of two spade blades (see overleaf). The aim is to improve the crumbliness of the subsoil without bringing it up to the surface, while keeping the most biologically active layer of soil (the topsoil) close to the young roots of the plants. This makes it a useful technique for an area where long-term, deeper-rooted plants, such as roses, shrubs, trees or fruit bushes, are to be grown. The benefits of double digging a plot can last for up to 15 years.

DOUBLE DIGGING TIP Avoid mixing the subsoil with the topsoil. If the two are mixed together, the fertility of the topsoil is diluted, rather than the fertility of the subsoil improved.

CLEANING TIP Clean the spade blade regularly, using a scraping tool such as a trowel. A clean spade slices through the soil more easily.

3

4

3 Dig a second trench, adjacent to the first, and throw the soil from the second trench into the first. (You can put manure or garden compost in the bottom of the trench first, if you wish to improve the soil's texture.) Turn each block of soil upside down as it is moved, so that the surface soil goes into the bottom of the trench to cover weeds and prevent new weed seeds from germinating.
4 Continue to dig trenches across the whole plot. Use the soil from the wheelbarrow to fill the last trench.

Double digging

You will need:
- garden line and about ten bamboo canes to mark out plot
- spade
- wheelbarrow
- fork to loosen soil
- pickaxe (optional)
- organic matter

1 Mark out the plot with canes and line, and remove the turf. Dig a trench 60cm wide and one spade deep, then place the soil from this trench in the wheelbarrow and take it to the far end of the plot, to be used to fill the final trench.

2 Fork over the subsoil in the base of the trench to the full depth of the fork's tines. You may need to use a pickaxe to break through very compacted soil.

3 Mix organic matter into the lower layer of soil to improve its structure and its drainage.

4 Using a spade, dig the topsoil from an adjacent second trench and throw it into the first, making sure that it gets turned over. (On new ground, or if the soil is not very fertile, you can incorporate a further dressing of compost or manure into the top layer of soil.) Fork over the bottom of the second trench in the same way as the first.

5 Repeat the process until the entire plot has been dug to a depth of about 50cm. Use the soil from the wheelbarrow to fill the last trench and finish the plot.

EVEN IF YOUR SOIL SEEMS IMPOSSIBLY DRY OR STICKY AND PRONE TO WATERLOGGING, IT IS POSSIBLE TO IMPROVE ITS DRAINAGE AND FERTILITY WITH THE ADDITION OF DIFFERENT MATERIALS AND THE APPLICATION OF APPROPRIATE TECHNIQUES AND DESIGNS.

Improving soil structure

Structure is the term given to the way the individual particles of soil bond together in clusters. If soil particles are fine, they are packed together so that water drains through slowly and the soil stays wet. By adding organic materials the structure can be improved by 'opening' the soil, allowing air and water to penetrate. If a soil is too open (drains too quickly), adding organic matter will help the soil particles to stick together more closely, allowing the soil to hold more water.

Why add organic matter?

Animal manures and fresh green plant waste provide small amounts of nutrients quite quickly, mainly nitrogen (N), phosphate (P) and potash (K). But fibrous and woody materials are much better for improving soil structure and 'opening' heavy soils, while on lighter, free-draining soils, they improve moisture retention. The ideal garden compost is a mixture of the two.

All bulky organic materials have low levels of nutrients when compared with inorganic concentrated fertilisers, but as the organic matter rots, it produces organic acids that dissolve nutrients already in the soil, making them available to plants.

■ **For green manure,** grow borage, comfrey, mustard, red clover or ryegrass and dig into the topsoil when the plants are six to eight weeks old. This will improve organic matter and nutrient levels, particularly nitrogen content, and smother germinating weeds.

ORGANIC MATTER TIP For maximum nutrient benefit from bulky organic materials such as manures, incorporate them into the soil when only partly rotted. The longer they are stored, the lower their nutritional value, because nutrients can leech away.

Improving soil fertility

A healthy, fertile soil needs a biologically active community of different organisms, capable of releasing and recycling nutrients so that plants can feed. For this to take place, there must be a balance between the amount of air in the soil (so that the beneficial organisms can live) and water (so that chemical changes can take place).

Time the application of manures, organic mulches or fertilisers so your plants gain maximum benefit, applying them either just as growth starts as a base dressing, or part-way through the growing cycle as a top dressing. Apply dry fertilisers to moist soil, as plants absorb nutrients in soluble form.

Bear in mind that over-feeding with high concentrations of fertilisers and manures can severely damage or kill plants by chemically burning their roots.

Adding lime

Lime raises the pH and neutralises soil acidity. This often benefits plant growth because many plant nutrients are more readily available when there is lime in the soil, and many soil organisms can only function well in a soil where there is lime. Ideally, lime should be added to the soil after digging but before it is cultivated down to a

You can remedy poor drainage by forking in organic material.

Adding mulches

ORGANIC MULCHES are used to:
- suppress weeds; the mulch needs to be at least 8cm deep to block out the light.
- reduce moisture loss; the mulch needs to be at least 5cm deep.
- improve soil fertility by encouraging high levels of biological activity while the organic material is broken down into the soil's upper layers.

FOR BEST RESULTS mulches should be spread evenly over the soil, and left to work their way into it. This is particularly important on heavy soil. If they are dug in, decomposition stops due to lack of oxygen. The soil structure may also be damaged by digging.

finer tilth – this ensures that the lime is evenly distributed. Apply in small quantities to avoid the risk of overliming.

Improving drainage

A soil that is both moisture-retentive and well-draining is achievable, but it is helpful to know how soil holds water – especially if you need to improve the drainage of a waterlogged area or lawn.

How soil holds water

A soil's ability to hold on to water varies. Some water is held in pores, the spaces between soil particles, but the main source for growing plants is capillary water, which clings to the surface of each soil particle.
- **Dry soils,** predominantly of sand and gravel, have large pores that allow them to drain quickly. Because they are made up of fewer, larger particles, they hold less capillary water and dry out rapidly.
- **Wet soils,** usually with a high clay content, are made up of lots of very small particles, giving them the potential to hold plenty of water. The pores in between are much smaller so water is held for longer, and the soil stays wet for prolonged periods.

Reasons for poor drainage

Poor drainage, where surplus water cannot drain away, can be caused by:
- **Surface compaction** or 'capping' occurs most commonly on silty soils where there is little organic matter or where not much vegetation covers the soil. If soil worked to a fine tilth becomes wet (through rain or irrigation), and then dries quickly, a crust or cap perhaps 1cm thick may form.
- **Deep compaction** is most commonly seen in the gardens of new houses where subsoil and topsoil have become mixed, and the soil mass has been pressed by heavy machinery. Deep cultivation through double digging is the only effective solution.
- **Hard pans** are compacted layers of soil, close to the surface. They stop water from draining well, producing waterlogged soil above. Causes can be cultivating wet soil or repeated walking over an area.
- **Heavy clay** has minute soil particles that may hold onto large volumes of water even where drains are present.

TESTING DRAINAGE TIP Dig a hole to about 50cm deep and 30–45cm in diameter (below). It will part-fill with water after 2 to 3 hours of rain but should empty within 48 hours as the water drains away. If it does not, you will have to take steps to correct your drainage.

Solutions to poor drainage

Techniques for improving drainage depend on the lie of the land, soil depth and soil type, and how much moisture the intended plants will tolerate. Avoid walking on waterlogged soil and don't try to cultivate it, as this makes the problem worse.

Installing a drainage system under lawns or cultivated areas may be the only effective solution to severe water-logging. Although initially disruptive, it should work well for up to 50 years. Even digging a shallow trench, filling it a third deep with a layer of aggregate then replacing the soil, will provide a solution for about ten years.

■ **Adding aggregate** Mixing in fine grit, horticultural sand or boiler ash helps to open up heavy soil. On very wet soils, cut narrow slits, about 8cm wide and 10cm deep, and fill them with aggregate.

■ **Varying the depth of cultivation** over different areas avoids creating a hard pan. Dig heavy soils in autumn before they become too wet, and leave as rough lumps over winter so that the wind and frost can dry them out and help to break the soil down to a finer tilth.

■ **Spiking lawns** using a hollow-tined aerator removes cores of soil about 1cm in diameter and up to 15cm long. This breaks through the compacted layer, allowing air in and moisture to evaporate. The holes can be filled by brushing in an open, sandy compost, which acts like a wick, drawing moisture up towards the surface.

■ **Growing plants on mounds** or ridges keeps most of the roots above the saturated soil. Raising the soil level in one part will also help it to dry out more quickly. Plants that prefer free-draining soil (like strawberries, lavenders and most herbs) will benefit from being grown 'high' even if the soil is not particularly wet.

■ **Raised beds** are ideal for heavy clay soils: water drains from the raised bed, allowing it to dry out ready for sowing or planting, and collects in the trenches where it evaporates.

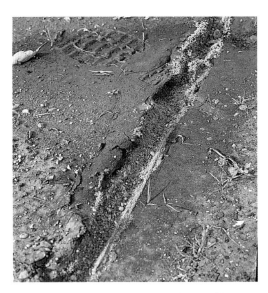

On a wet soil, make narrow slits and then fill them with fine-particled aggregate.

For raised beds, dig a series of trenches 20–30cm deep, placing the soil in between them to create beds about 1.2m wide.

■ **Installing a land drain** means that the upper soil layers, at least, will be drier. A sloping narrow trench is dug from the top of the garden, across the land towards the lowest point. Porous clay or perforated plastic pipes are placed within a porous layer (ash or gravel) before the trench is refilled with soil. (Clay pipes are about 40cm long and plastic drains are bought in flexible coils up to 30m long.)

Conserving water in the soil

■ Adding organic matter to a light sandy soil can improve its water-holding capacity by 25 per cent in the first year and 60 per cent in the second year. It will also open up a clay soil, which tends to dry out and bake hard in summer, improving its water-holding capacity. Annual applications are essential to maintain these improvements.

■ An organic mulch of up to 5cm deep will reduce surface evaporation and considerably improve the conservation of water in the soil.

GATHER UP YOUR GARDEN AND KITCHEN WASTE AND RECYCLE IT TO PROVIDE A FREE SUPPLY OF NUTRIENTS FOR THE GARDEN. COMPOSTING IS NOT DIFFICULT OR SMELLY – IT IS A MEANS OF SPEEDING UP THE NATURAL PROCESS OF DECOMPOSITION.

How composting works

Left to itself, a heap of garden waste will warm up in the centre as the softer, greener ingredients start to ferment and rot. This warmth encourages worms and other organisms to feed on the waste and, in time, turn it into a crumbly, sweet-smelling substance rich in plant foods that holds water like a sponge.

Making compost

The secret of making good compost is to mix quick-rotting green waste and tougher fibrous materials in roughly equal amounts, and keep them warm and moist in a container, preferably insulated, as the beneficial aerobic bacteria need warmth, moisture and air in order to break down waste. A lid ensures that the compost does not become too wet or dry out, and helps to retain much of the heat, accelerating decay.

■ **Add a mixture of materials** in 15cm layers, or fork them into the heap. If you

Recycling perennial weeds

The roots of perennial weeds can survive and even multiply in a compost heap, while seeds and spores on mature or diseased weeds will only be killed if the temperature is sufficiently high. You can compost these weeds separately in a black plastic bag, mixed with a bucketful of mowings to help build up heat. Tie the bag tightly and leave for at least six months over the summer months, longer over winter, after which the contents can safely be added to the compost heap.

have a lot of one type of material stack it to one side and cover with black plastic sheeting until there is sufficient variation to mix together. Large quantities of grass cuttings will not go slimy if mixed with torn crumpled paper or egg boxes, while fibrous waste will rot faster mixed with grass cuttings, nettle tops or comfrey leaves.

■ **Continue to add waste** until the container is full, although the level will sink as the contents rot.

■ **Check that the heap is moist;** water it occasionally in hot weather.

■ **Cover the top with an old blanket**, piece of carpet or a layer of straw if there is no lid, and leave to rot for at least six months in summer – rotting will tend to slow down over winter.

Shredding woody waste

Thick stems and tough prunings take years to decompose unless chopped into fragments in a shredder. Petrol or electric

In six to twelve months, raw kitchen and garden waste (left) will have rotted down into a crumbly mass at the bottom of the heap (above) – a valuable source of organic matter.

models are available, usually capable of dealing with bundles of plant stems and branches up to 2–3cm in diameter. Make sure that the blades are kept sharp and don't overload the machine. Adding the fibrous shreddings to the compost heap will aerate the mixture and help it to break down much more quickly.

Resolving problems

■ **Unpleasant smells** Turn or fork the heap, working in fibrous materials such as torn newspapers and straw.

■ **A dry heap that does not rot** Water itwell or, if the contents are mostly fibrous, mix in soft green waste such as grass cuttings.

■ **A cold wet heap** Turn or remix the contents, adding plenty of fibrous material. In cold weather, cover with old blankets, a piece of carpet, old sacking or a large piece of bubble wrap.

■ **Flies** They are harmless and part of the decomposition process, but if to discourage them, cover the bin with a close-fitting lid.

Compost ingredients

Quick-rotting materials
These provide the active ingredients for a compost heap.

■ **Soft, sappy, green waste** such as weeds, young plants, soft (not woody) prunings, fruit and vegetable peelings.

■ **Lawn cuttings and nettles** – these heat up very fast, and are used as accelerators to stimulate a dry compost heap into life.

■ **Horse and poultry manure**, tea and coffee grounds, and used litter such as hay from small pets (including rabbits, guinea pigs and pigeons).

Slow-rotting materials
These add bulk and prevent the softer materials from turning into a wet and evil-smelling mass.

■ **Fibrous materials** such as shredded paper and card products, straw, vegetable

An electric shredder makes quick work of chopping up thick plant stems. For safety, wear gloves and face and ear protectors.

stems, leaves, eggshells and soft hedge prunings.

■ **Thick stems and woody material:** these need to be chopped or crushed with a spade, or shredded.

Do not use: meat and fish scraps; cat and dog faeces; plastic and synthetic fibres; coal ashes; wood, metal or glass; diseased plant material; perennial and seeding weeds.

Composting autumn leaves
You can mix small amounts of leaves into the compost heap, but large quantities are better stacked separately. Leaf-mould is slower to make than compost but should need no attention after you have packed the leaves into netting cages or plastic bags.

Making leaf-mould in bags

Rake up fallen leaves after rain and pack into black plastic bags; tie the tops and punch a few holes in the sides. Stack the bags in a corner of the garden for a year while the leaves decay.

COMPOST TIP For faster leaf-mould, spread the leaves on the lawn and use a rotary mower to chop into fragments before bagging up. The grass cuttings help the leaves to decay faster.

Compost containers

Although garden waste can be left in a heap, it is tidier and more efficient to contain it in a bin. Various models are available, or you can easily make your own wooden compost containers. Timber is one of the best materials for a compost bin as it is an efficient insulator and you can recycle old pallets or wooden boards in its construction. The minimum sized container to make sure you get sufficient heat at the centre measures 1 x 1 x 1m and the loose front panels allow you easy access. Attach a second bin alongside the first if you have enough space, so that the contents of the first mature while you fill up the other.

Ready-made compost bins

Buying a ready-made compost bin is the easiest way to get started with compost. They come in all shapes and sizes and most work reasonably well, but some designs make better and quicker compost than others. They also range widely in price – where cost is the main factor, try contacting

Making leaf mould

1 Rake up autumn leaves, preferably after rain. Stack them outdoors in a simple low enclosure. (You can make one easily by driving four stakes into the ground and wrapping them round with chicken netting.) Tread down the leaves to make room for more. Leave the heap open, or cover with old carpet or sacking.

2 The level of leaf-mould will fall dramatically as the leaves decay, and you can sometimes combine two heaps into one after a year. By this time, the partially decomposed leaf-mould makes an excellent soil conditioner and mulching material.

3 If you allow leaf-mould to rot for two years, you can sieve out the finer material and add it to potting composts and top-dressings for lawns.

Worm compost

Small amounts of kitchen waste can be recycled in a worm bin or 'wormery' to produce a very rich compost that you can use as a fertiliser for potting mixtures, lawn top-dressings, fruit or large container plants. Kits are available supplying everything you need, including the worms. The container usually has a facility for draining off a concentrated solution that you can dilute and use as a liquid feed.

A wormery can run for a year or more before it is full, depending on how much it is 'fed', and you can remove the finished compost from the bottom of most proprietary bins.

Make sure the bin has a well-fitting lid. There is no need for the bin to have air-holes. Enough air is introduced every time you add materials, and it is possible to produce excellent compost without air if you add the right materials in the right proportions. Bins with gaps in the sides will need the materials turning regularly to ensure even rotting.

Alternative containers

■ **Wire-mesh cage** with four corner posts and lined with cardboard or straw.
■ **Large plastic barrel** with 2–3cm holes drilled 30cm apart around the base and halfway up the sides.
■ **Proprietary square or conical plastic bin** with a close-fitting lid.
■ **Compost tumbler**, a barrel that is turned daily for fast results, mounted on a frame.
■ **Old beehives** with removable wooden slats.
■ **Whole builders' pallets** make excellent 'instant' compost bins set on end and lashed together. For extra insulation, fill the gaps with straw or newspaper.

your local authority, as most offer either free or heavily subsidised bins. Otherwise, expect to pay between £45 and £100, depending on construction and size. The choice of design of council-supplied composters is fairly limited, but if you intend to choose your own, here are a few points to bear in mind.
■ **A round bin** takes up more unproductive space than a square or rectangular one. Several square bins can be positioned side by side and will keep each other warm.
■ **Dark colours** absorb heat more readily, so organic materials break down quicker.
■ **The ingredients in the centre** heat up and stay hot more efficiently than those around the edge, so the larger the bin, the better it is at making good compost.
■ **Ensure there is an easy way** of extracting the compost when it is ready. Inexpensive, round bins are usually bigger at the bottom than the top, so can be slid up to access the compost, more expensive ones should have a door somewhere near the base.
■ **The thicker the walls**, the hotter the compost will get. Thin plastic will cool off when the outside temperature drops. Wood is a good insulator, but rots in time. Some bins are made of twin-wall plastic sheets, which work in a similar way to double glazing, and produce compost more quickly.

Although many alternatives are available, timber is one of the best materials for a compost bin and blends well into the garden.

ALL PLANTS NEED FEEDING IN ORDER TO PERFORM AT THEIR BEST AND REMAIN HEALTHY. IN A GARDEN PLANTS GROW CLOSELY IN A LIMITED SPACE, WHICH TAKES MORE OUT OF THE SOIL THAN GOES BACK IN NATURALLY. THE SITUATION IS COMPOUNDED BY THE REMOVAL OF PLANT DEBRIS WHICH WOULD OTHERWISE ROT AND RETURN NUTRIENTS TO THE SOIL.

The addition of organic material helps to create a well-balanced soil and increase its fertility. Organic materials are those derived from animal matter or plant debris.

■ **Manures** are generally regarded as those with an organic origin, such as dung, garden compost and leaf-mould, which break down into humus. They must be well rotted.

■ **Mulches** are applied to the surface of soil in order to enrich it, suppress annual weeds and help to keep the soil warm and moist. Well-rotted organic material used as a mulch, rather than being dug into the soil, breaks down more slowly and reduces the speed at which nutrients are leached.

■ **Fertilisers** provide little or no humus, but have concentrated salts – for example, superphosphate of lime, sulphate of ammonia and sulphate of potash – which supplement the soil's own nutrients.

If you have a large area of lawn to feed, a fertiliser spreader can save time and help to give an even coverage of nutrients.

Types of fertiliser

Both artificial and organic fertilisers supplement the three principal nutrients essential to plant growth: nitrogen, phosphorus and potassium. These chemicals can be bought separately or combined in a general-purpose fertiliser such as Growmore which consists of equal amounts of nitrogen, phosphorus and potassium, in the form of sulphate of ammonia, superphosphate of lime and sulphate of potash.

■ **Nitrogen** produces growth. Too much gives lush, leafy soft growth; too little results in small yellow leaves and lack of vigour.

■ **Phosphorus** is important to seedlings and in the formation of seeds. Too little turns leaves dull purple and slows down growth; too much causes premature ripening.

■ **Potassium** enhances flower colour; it also improves resistance to pests and diseases and hardens the tissues.

Easy fertiliser application

For easy and accurate distribution of nutrients, make your own applicator using two small plastic pots of the same size, placed one inside the other with the drainage holes just offset to leave small gaps. Fill it with granular fertiliser and simply shake the pot to distribute the fertiliser evenly.

■ **Other nutrients, called trace elements,** are also necessary for healthy growth, but in tiny quantities. They are present in a number of fertiliser formulations, including those based on seaweed. Trace-element deficiencies can often be remedied with a foliar feed (see below). Slow-release formulas, such as Osmacote and Vitex Q4, also contain trace elements, and are ideal on permanent plantings.

As well as being sold as powder, pellets or granules (for slow release), fertilisers are available in liquid form which can be applied to the roots of a plant for rapid absorption. Alternatively, they are sold as foliar feeds, applied with a watering can and rapidly absorbed through the leaves. Liquid fertilisers come as a balanced feed for general purposes, or as mixtures for specific plants, such as roses and tomatoes.

Fertilisers must be applied according to the manufacturer's instruction or the result may be counterproductive.

It is essential to wear gloves to protect your hands whenever you are handling fertilisers in dry form.

Slow-release fertiliser pellets supply food continuously over several months throughout the growing season.

Organic mulches and fertilisers

Bark (composted)

■ **Characteristics** Bark increases the soil's humus content, protects roots, suppresses weeds and retains moisture. It also increases the acidity of the soil. Softwood bark is more acidic and contains fewer nutrients than hardwood bark.

■ **Source** Garden centres and mail-order companies. Use only commercially bagged supplies which have been detoxified. Avoid cheap bulk supplies.

■ **How to apply** Surface mulch and soil-texture improver. Use with a nitrogen-rich fertiliser. As a surface mulch, spread it 5cm thick. As a soil conditioner dig in 4-8kg per m².

Bonemeal

■ **Characteristics** Contains 20-25% phosphorus and 3-6% nitrogen. A good slow-release fertiliser.

■ **Source** Garden centres and by mailorder. Good for use in autumn and winter.

■ **How to apply** Use 140-200g per m². To apply as a liquid manure, add to water, stir well and apply at once.

Coir/coconut fibre

■ **Characteristics** Good moisture-holding capacity but tends to dry out quickly on the surface. Little nutrient value.

■ **Source** Garden centres and by mail order.

■ **How to apply** Use as an alternative to peat when making up composts for potting and propagation. For ecological reasons coir is not recommended for large-scale use as a soil conditioner or mulch.

Dried blood

■ **Characteristics** Has about 12% nitrogen content. One of the fastest-acting fertilisers. Good for spring and summer.

■ **Source** Sold in bags at garden centres and by mail order.

How to apply Before sowing or planting in spring or summer and to plants in growth. Apply 35-100g per m². It is not fully soluble but it can be used as a liquid manure if stirred well and applied at once at a rate of 15-30g per 4.5 litres of water.

Farmyard manure

Characteristics Well-balanced plant food, containing nitrogen, phosphorus and potassium. Avoid on acid soils. Horse manure is richer, dryer and more open-textured than pig or cattle manure. When mixed with straw and rotted, it is a soil improver, source of organic matter and protective, weed-suppressing mulch.

Source Farms, stables (when it is often mixed with straw) and garden centres. Quality varies according to the animals' diet and how manure is stored. Ideally, buy it fresh from a farm and add it to the compost heap to rot. Proprietary brands are an acceptable substitute, but are concentrated and expensive.

How to apply Use decayed or composted manure as a top dressing – either neat or mixed with an equal measure of soil.

If you live in the countryside, it may be relatively easy to obtain manure from local farmers. But be careful about how you apply it; it is not suitable for all crops.

Apply it only in spring or summer – one wheelbarrow of well-rotted manure to each 10m² per year.

Fish, blood and bone

Characteristics About 3% nitrogen and 8% phosphorus.
Source Garden centres and by mail order.
How to apply In late winter or early spring, use as a general-purpose soil dressing before putting plants in a bed or sowing seeds. Apply 140g per m².

Garden compost

Characteristics Soil improver and source of organic matter. As a mulch, it retains moisture and protects roots from frost. Dug in, it improves soil texture.
Source See pages 36-37.
How to apply Spread it 5cm thick as a mulch. To improve the soil dig in generously, as with farmyard manure.

Green manure

Characteristics Organic material rich in nitrogen, such as mustard, rape and clover. Dug in it improves soil fertility; as a mulch it retains moisture and protects roots from frost. Use it to supplement manure or fertiliser. Also grow it as a winter ground cover to prevent nutrients from being washed through the soil.
Source Sow your own where it is to be used, following the instructions on the packet.
How to apply Sow in autumn. Cut down to ground level when 20cm high, and dig into the soil two days later while still green. As a mulch, cut and lay it 5cm thick over soil.

Hoof and horn meal

Characteristics Contains 12-14% nitrogen. Coarse-ground meal is slower acting than the finely ground kind.

Source Garden centres and by mail order, but expensive.

How to apply Apply in spring and summer at 90g per m².

Leaf-mould

Characteristics A nutritious mulch, but needs anchoring with sand, bark or netting. Also good as a soil-texture improver. Compost separately from other organic material for at least a year.

Source Garden centres or homemade.

How to apply Use leaf-mould with a nitrogen-rich fertiliser, which will help to break it down. As a mulch spread a layer 2.5cm thick. As a soil improver, dig in 2.5kg per m².

Mushroom compost

Characteristics Has nitrogen, phosphorus and potassium, according to nature of compost. Good improver of soil texture. Contains lime, so do not use it on alkaline soil or on lime-hating plants.

Source Available from garden centres or mushroom growers.

How to apply As a surface mulch at any time. Or dig in up to 11kg per m². A good way of raising pH if the soil is acid.

Peat

Characteristics Peat has little value as plant food, but for several decades has been a valuable ingredient in composts used for propagation. It can also be used to bulk up soil-based compost when it is used in large containers or small raised beds. Difficult to re-wet once it has dried out.

Source Garden centres and by mail order.

How to apply To make your own compost for raising cuttings, mix 50% peat with 50% horticultural sand (measured by volume). Large-scale use of peat is not recommended because its extraction destroys unique wildlife habitats. There are a number of natural alternatives to peat including coir and composted bark.

Seaweed meal

Characteristics Contains about 2% nitrogen, 2% phosphorus, and is rich in trace elements. Acts as a soil conditioner and encourages plant growth. Particularly useful on poor soil.

Source Garden centres and by mail order.

How to apply Use in autumn as a general-purpose fertiliser/soil conditioner, or three months before planting, at 140g per m².

Wood ash

Characteristics An alkaline material and good source of potassium. Amount of potassium varies between 15% and 4%. Keep it dry to prevent nutrients from being washed out, or add it to the compost heap.

Source Bonfires or wood-burning stoves.

How to apply Use wood ash to reduce acidity of soil. May be used at any time of the year. Apply up to 140g per m². When using as a liquid add 15g of wood ash per 4.5 litres of water.

Inorganic fertilisers

Phosphate of potash

Characteristics Roughly 50% phosphorus, 35% potassium. Soluble fertiliser and highly concentrated. Good liquid fertiliser to use during the growth phase.

Source Garden centres but expensive.

How to apply At any time of year. As a liquid fertiliser use up to 15g per 4.5 litres of water. Or dig in 140g per m².

Rock phosphate

Characteristics Contains about 3% nitrogen and 20% phosphorus. It is a slow-acting fertiliser which is used as an alternative to bone meal.

Source Available from most garden centres.

How to apply Use in the same way as you would bone meal. Apply in autumn or winter – either before planting or raked into the soil as a top dressing – at 120g per m².

Sulphate of ammonia
■ **Characteristics** Contains 20% nitrogen and is used in many compound fertilisers. Fairly rapid action. Good on limy soils but increases the acidity of acid soils. Must be stored in a dry place.
■ **Source** Garden centres.
■ **How to apply** Use in spring or early summer. Never mix it with lime as ammonia gas will be released, wasting nitrogen. Apply up to 75g per m^2 of soil. As a liquid manure, use 15g per 4.5 litres of water.

Sulphate of magnesium (Epsom salts)
■ **Characteristics** Has 10% magnesium, is soluble and quick-acting, so best used as a foliar feed. Less a fertiliser than a supplement of magnesium.
■ **Source** Garden centres.
■ **How to apply** Use in spring and summer. Apply up to 75g per m^2. As a liquid spray use 15g per 4.5 litres of water.

Sulphate of potash
■ **Characteristics** Contains 48% potassium. Holds well in the soil.
■ **Source** Garden centres.
■ **How to apply** Use at any time of the year. Apply up to 140g per m^2. As a liquid, use 15g per 4.5 litres of water.

Superphosphate of lime
■ **Characteristics** Contains 12-18% phosphoric acid. Quick-acting, reasonably soluble fertiliser. Despite its name, it will not increase soil alkalinity as the lime is a form of gypsum.
■ **Source** Garden centres.
■ **How to apply** Use alone or mixed with other fertilisers in spring or early summer. Apply up to 140g per m^2. As a liquid, mix 30g per 4.5 litres of water.

Gardening the organic way
Organic gardening is gardening with the wider environment in mind. It relies on natural methods to control pests and to build up the fertility of the soil. Organic gardening recycles farm and garden wastes rather than disposing of them in ways that would pollute the environment.

Enriching the soil
The starting point for effective organic gardening is to create soil that holds moisture but drains well and encourages extensive root growth. It will provide plants with a balanced, slow-release diet to promote steady growth. The plants will then be less prone to attack by pests and diseases than chemically fed plants.

The ground should be cultivated as little as possible. Don't walk on the soil when it is wet, and keep it covered with growing plants or a mulch wherever possible.
■ **Soil improvers** To improve the soil, use garden compost and leaf-mould – made by recycling kitchen and garden waste – augmented with brought-in ingredients such as animal manure and extra autumn leaves. Do not use manures derived from intensive farming systems because of the higher levels of food additives, antibiotics and other chemicals.
■ **Garden compost,** well-rotted manure, mushroom compost, hay, seaweed, cocoa shells and grass cuttings are all rich in nutrients. Use them only during spring or summer. If they are applied when plants are not actively growing, their goodness will be leached from the soil and wasted.
■ **Low-nutrient materials,** such as straw, leaf-mould, composted bark and prunings chopped up in a shredder, may be applied at any time of the year and in any quantity. If possible, use one wheelbarrow load of well-rotted farmyard manure or two barrow loads of garden compost to each $10m^2$ of ground each year.
■ **Organic soil improvers** can be used either as a surface mulch or mixed with the top 15cm layer of soil. A mulch acts as an insulating layer and should be applied to warm, wet soil only.

Making organic liquid manure

In organic gardening the aim is to feed the soil, which feeds the plants. Although liquid feeds do not strictly comply with this aim because they supply the plant more or less directly, their use can be essential when plants are grown in pots, tubs and other containers. And you can make your own.

1 Shear off the fresh young growth of comfrey or nettles in spring, using a pair of garden shears.

2 Pack the leaves into a net bag and tie it at the top.

3 Suspend the bag in a tank or bucket of water for 10-14 days, occasionally squeezing the bag. Dilute the resulting liquor to look like weak tea before applying.

■ **Unrotted soil improvers,** such as hay, straw, seaweed and grass cuttings, can be composted first or added straight to the garden. If not composted, use as a mulch.

Green manures

Plants grown specifically to benefit the soil's fertility and structure are called green manures. They may be dug into the soil or cut and used as a mulch, and are especially useful in the vegetable garden. Grazing rye, for example, can be grown in winter as a soil cover to prevent plant nutrients being washed out. It also improves the structure of the soil and prevents weeds. Other plants used as green manures are clover, *Phacelia tanacetifolia*, mustard, fenugreek and winter tares. All can be bought as seeds.

Slow-release fertilisers and mineral supplements

Fertilisers of natural origin – plant, animal and rock – release their nutrients slowly. They can be used to adjust a major deficiency, or where compost and other materials are not available in sufficient quantities. They include hoof and horn, fish blood and bone meal, rock phosphate, dolomite limestone (to raise alkalinity), vinash (a by-product of the wine industry), seaweed meal, calcified seaweed, crab shells, gypsum and sulphur.

Designing your garden

GIVING SOME THOUGHT TO WHAT YOU WANT OUT OF YOUR GARDEN BEFORE YOU START
SERIOUS WORK WILL SAVE YOU TIME, MONEY AND LABOUR. A SUCCESSFUL GARDEN TAKES
TIME TO DEVELOP, SO DO NOT BE TEMPTED TO RUSH THE JOB. A GARDEN CREATED IN A
HURRY MAY TAKE AS MUCH WORK TO PUT RIGHT AS STARTING FROM NEW.

If you have a brand new garden, you can
start designing with a clean sheet. Most of
us take over someone else's efforts, though,
and you may be tempted to tear everything
out and start again. If you can bear to wait,
you may be surprised at what appears as
the seasons unfold, and at the end of the
year you may have very different ideas
of how to progress. Keep the plot
well tended and weed free until
you are sure you want to make
alterations; this will help you to
familiarise yourself with its good and
bad points as the year progresses.

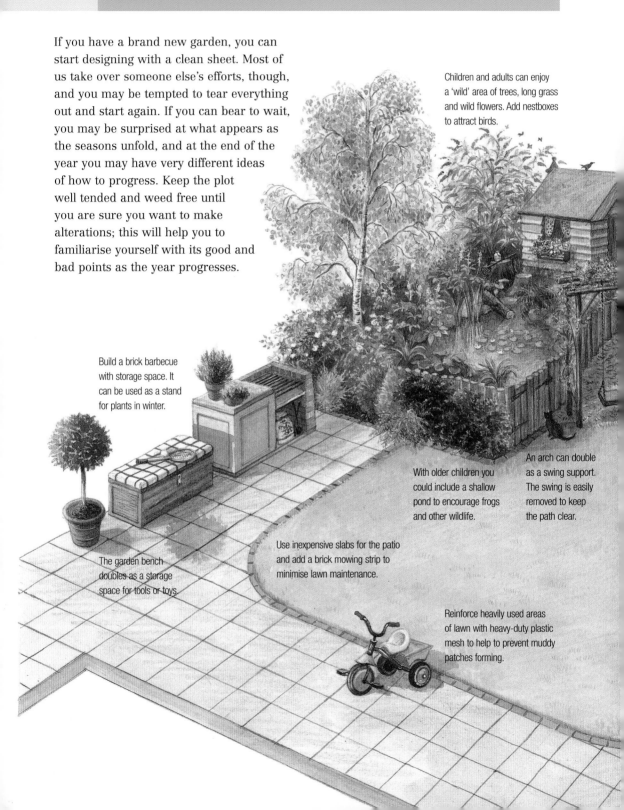

Children and adults can enjoy
a 'wild' area of trees, long grass
and wild flowers. Add nestboxes
to attract birds.

Build a brick barbecue
with storage space. It
can be used as a stand
for plants in winter.

With older children you
could include a shallow
pond to encourage frogs
and other wildlife.

An arch can double
as a swing support.
The swing is easily
removed to keep
the path clear.

The garden bench
doubles as a storage
space for tools or toys.

Use inexpensive slabs for the patio
and add a brick mowing strip to
minimise lawn maintenance.

Reinforce heavily used areas
of lawn with heavy-duty plastic
mesh to help to prevent muddy
patches forming.

Observe and research

■ **Look at what thrives already** in the garden, and those of your neighbours. Similarly, make a mental note of what does not seem to do well. For instance, if rhododendrons and camellias burgeon with health, you will know that the local soil is acid and you will be able to grow azaleas, heathers and other plants that require these conditions. But if you do not see a certain group of plants in surrounding plots, or the few that grow there look sorry for themselves, you can be fairly certain that they will not like yours, either.

■ **Spend time at a good nursery** or garden centre without making any purchases. Most now have cultivation labels either over the beds or on the plants themselves. Take special note of soil requirements and

Children can play in their own 'jungle zone' in a thicket of shrubs. Make a path of stepping stones so they can forge a way through.

Give children their own patch of garden where they can raise quick-growing plants such as sunflowers, gourds, nasturtiums and radishes.

Fit the children's sandpit with a bamboo roller blind to protect it from the weather and cats. When it is outgrown, it can be coverted into a raised herb bed.

A FAMILY GARDEN Families make many conflicting demands on a garden. Children need space to play and keep pets, while adults want an attractive environment in which to relax and to entertain friends. The design of a family garden needs to reflect these different requirements and be flexible enough to evolve as the family grows up. Try to look at your garden as a whole, and go for features that are either dual-purpose or easily adapted to take on a new use with time.

A LOW-MAINTENANCE GARDEN This kind of garden works well for people who enjoy their garden but do not want to spend a great deal of time looking after it. The diagonal lines make the most of the plot's narrow shape and maintenance-free paving materials and easy-care plants keep down the workload.

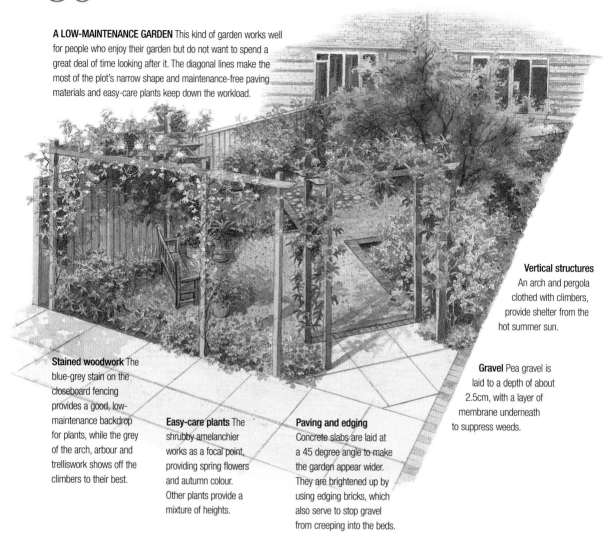

Vertical structures
An arch and pergola clothed with climbers, provide shelter from the hot summer sun.

Gravel Pea gravel is laid to a depth of about 2.5cm, with a layer of membrane underneath to suppress weeds.

Stained woodwork The blue-grey stain on the closeboard fencing provides a good, low-maintenance backdrop for plants, while the grey of the arch, arbour and trelliswork shows off the climbers to their best.

Easy-care plants The shrubby amelanchier works as a focal point, providing spring flowers and autumn colour. Other plants provide a mixture of heights.

Paving and edging Concrete slabs are laid at a 45 degree angle to make the garden appear wider. They are brightened up by using edging bricks, which also serve to stop gravel from creeping into the beds.

eventual size, as well as habit, flowering times and any other features that immediately catch your eye. Keep a notebook or diary that you can refer to once you start serious planning.

■ Find out if there is a local radio gardening programme in your area. Here you should get 'hands on' advice by practical gardeners who know what grows locally.

■ Buy a good gardening encyclopedia or join your local library and borrow some books on all aspects of garden design and cultivation.

■ Send for some good nursery and seed catalogues.

The importance of good preparation

Whether you are redesigning the whole garden, giving it a general makeover, or just starting a new project, thorough preparation of ground and soil is essential.

Dig out all weeds and unwanted plants, or, if the area is very overgrown, treat with a weedkiller such as glyphosate, which does not poison the soil so you will be able to replant once the weeds are completely dead. Leave bare ground unplanted for a while to allow any weed seeds to grow, then deal with them as above. Dig over the soil to a depth of at least 30cm and add plenty of farmyard manure or garden compost, so new plants can get their roots into something good.

Though it may not be possible everything on your list, but you can then consider ways round the problem. For example, you may not be able to have a vegetable patch, but you can still grow a reasonable number in raised beds on the patio. Fruit can be trained on trellises and walls, mixing different types of plants means you can include many of your favourites in a single border, a lawn can also be a children's play area if you choose a tough grass. Dogs, especially, need to be planned for carefully; if you have a bitch, you may find decorative chippings more practical than a lawn. A dog will lift his leg indiscriminately, and will soon kill the lower branches of evergreen shrubs and conifers, so plan you garden to keep anything well out of his way.

Think about available time

This will depend on what is actually available, and how you want to split it up between gardening, other necessary jobs, and other leisure activities. Never take on more than you can cope with – you can always increase your gardening workload later if you want to. If you go away a lot, you may like to consider keeping containers –

hanging baskets, window boxes, tubs and troughs – to a minimum, or install an automatic watering system.

Costing the project

A garden can be as economical or as costly as you wish to make it. If money is tight, start with the basic essentials as you see them – perhaps paths, a lawn and a tool shed and a flowerbed – and lay out the garden so that you can add other items from your wish list later. If you are experienced at DIY you can save a great deal on hard landscaping, but bringing in a professional may save you even more in the long run. Think about cheaper alternatives which may be replaced easily with something more substantial in the future. Hard landscaping – walling and paving – will take the bulk of your budget, especially if you employ a professional to do the job and want something complicated. Perhaps you could economise by starting off with gravel paths you can lay yourself. These can be replaced easily by your chosen bricks or decorative slabs at a later date if finances allow. Both finishes are attractive, so you can still look out on something pleasing in the meantime. Or maybe you would like to build a wall? Try starting off with a functional fence, then graduate to a wall when funds recover.

Decide what you want

Make a list of all the features you wish to incorporate. These may include:

▦ Patio	▦ Vegetables	▦ Pond or water feature
▦ Paths	▦ Fruit	▦ Spring and summer bulbs
▦ Lawn	▦ Herbs	▦ Climbing and other wall plants
▦ Fence	▦ Annuals and bedding plants	▦ Containers
▦ Walls	▦ Flowers for cutting	▦ Greenhouse and/or
▦ Hedges	▦ Shrubs	cold frame
▦ Working/dustbin area	▦ Roses	▦ Summerhouse
▦ Children's garden	▦ Ornamental trees	▦ Shed
or play area	▦ Herbaceous perennials	▦ Statuary
▦ Drying area	▦ Alpines/rockery	▦ Facilities for pets

Drawing up a plan

Even if you are only designing one area or border, it is helpful to draw a scale plan. This will show you what will fit in, and the best places for everything you want to include. It will also help you to set out your garden accurately when you are ready.

You will need

■ **A tape** to measure the garden or the part of it you wish to design (and for setting it out from the plan)

■ **A compass** to check the north point (if you do not have a compass you can find west which is where the sun sets on 21 March in the UK)

■ **A large sheet of drawing paper** (squared or graph paper makes it easier to draw in the features and scale them off when you are ready to transfer the design to the garden)

■ **A pair of compasses** to define the spread of plants you wish to include

■ **A pencil** and an eraser

■ **Coloured pencils** or pens

What you need to include

Your plan should show all boundaries and internal divisions, permanent features such as existing pergolas, sheds, trees and mature shrubs and the position of all buildings adjoining the garden, which will help you to think about shade, rain shadows, root competition and drip. When measuring, take as many check measurements as possible (for instance, if you are wanting to show the position of a tree, take measurements from other objects so you can mark the correct place of the tree on the plan with your pair of compasses).

Take a critical look at your garden from all the windows overlooking it, as well as from any proposed sitting area and/or summerhouse, and decide on any good or bad views that you might want to emphasise or block. Mark these on the plan at the outset. Choose a scale to correspond with the squares on your graph paper. When you come to implementing your design, you can transfer many of the measurements from the drawing to the ground simply by counting squares.

Make sure your measurements are accurate before you begin as you will be using your plan for estimating quantities of materials for hard landscaping, grass seed or turf and the number and kinds of plants to buy and if you intend to get professional help the tradesmen will need it for quotations. It may take some time to get the design as you want it and you may get a better idea of how the garden will look if before you finish you colour in certain areas, especially the plants, with coloured pens or pencils.

Once you are entirely satisfied with your drawing, get it copied so you can use the copy in the garden, while keeping your original clean. Remember to keep your plan in a safe place after the garden is finished. You may need to refer to it in the future if you lose a label, and should you move home, the incoming occupant will find it useful to identify all the plants he or she is taking over.

1 Shredders reduce garden rubbish to a mulch that can be spread on beds and borders.

2 Mulches can keep borders and beds weed-free for a whole year.

AN EASY-CARE FRONT GARDEN A front garden is the gateway to your home and is viewed from both the inside and the outside. As is shown by this example, work can be kept to an absolute minimum without compromising on impact. In fact, often the simpler the design, the more aesthetic it can be.

Abide by the law

Contact your local authority when modifying your front garden. You may need permission for:

▓ **Walls and fences** To build a wall, fence or non-living plant support adjoining a public road higher than 90cm. There are no restrictions on hedges, but you may have to cut back vegetation that gets in the way of a road.

▓ **Terracing** You will need to submit plans and specifications for terracing which has a retaining wall more than 1.2m high and which is to be built within 3.5m of the road.

▓ **Roadside verges** You will need a licence to cultivate the verge outside your house. The planning department may limit what kind of plants you can grow.

Creating a 'crossover' If you are building a new driveway, ask the council to flatten the curb outside your house to allow for easy access. You will have to pay for them to do this.

3 A pressure washer keeps paving pristine; a path cleaner, with moss and algae controls, has a more lasting effect.

4 Make the access to your front door direct, because meandering paths will be ignored by visitors.

5 Make sure that any ornaments or containers in the front garden are secured to prevent theft.

6 Gravel is quickly and easily kept free of weeds by applying a path weedkiller in spring, or by raking occasionally to disturb and kill weed seedlings.

A NETWORK OF PATHS IS ESSENTIAL TO GET YOU FROM ONE PART OF THE GARDEN TO ANOTHER, OTHERWISE A WELL USED WALKWAY WOULD END UP A MUDDY MESS. A PATH DOES NOT HAVE TO BE MERELY FUNCTIONAL, AND CHOSEN CAREFULLY, CAN ADD MUCH TO THE OVERALL APPEARANCE.

Designing a path

When you start planning your path, you need to take account of who will use it, and for what purpose as well as how much it will cost. For instance, gravel is comparatively inexpensive, easy to lay, and comparatively low-maintenance, but if you intend to wheel barrows along it, or if wheelchairs or baby buggies are likely to run over it, gravel will be a very difficult surface to negotiate. A grass path is as easy to provide and maintain as a lawn, but if it will get a lot of use, it will more often than not be a mud-bath in winter and worn down to bare earth in dry spells in summer. Grass, although pleasing to look at, should only be considered if the path will only get light traffic. For the majority of circumstances, some kind of hard finish is the most practical.

The path should, in most instances, take the shortest route from A to B. Keep the design as simple as possible, avoiding sharp bends or curves that tempt the user to take a short cut, and make it wide enough for two people to pass if necessary. Where the path crosses a lawn, an alternative is to sink stepping-stones in the grass so the mower can cut over the top of them. This will reinforce the grass where it is walked on most, without taking up a lot of ground with hard landscaping.

Choosing a material

Apart from the practicalities outlined above, the material of which a garden path is made is mainly a personal choice. The advantages of gravel or stone chippings may be outweighed by their disadvantages – they are not the easiest finish to negotiate, they need regular weeding once the path has been down a while, and they can tread off

onto the surrounding garden. Timber paths are fashionable, but easily become slippery and have a finite life. Chipped bark should only be considered as a temporary measure as it needs regular topping up and the birds throw it everywhere. Asphalt is a hard-wearing surface but is best laid by a professional, and its appearance lends itself more to driveways than the normal garden

Top Squarish paving stones slightly offset and laid on gravel, make a casual path for an abundant flower border.
Below A cobblestone path laid in rectangles is a walkway through an avenue of trees and flowering shrubs.

Front garden paths

Front garden paths

■ **Functional paths** Paths from garden gate to front door should take the shortest route if they are going to be used by casual visitors. They can be made to look more attractive by introducing gentle curves or by using a variety of paving materials (see opposite).

■ **Decorative paths** In large gardens a second path can be used to meander through the garden and provide easy access to each area. It can be a continuous 'snake' of paving or stepping stones, or a combination of both.

path. In the majority of cases, a hard surface – concrete, slabs or blocks – is by far the most practical and enduring. Pattern imprint concrete has a more natural appearance than the somewhat austere concrete path, but has to be laid professionally.

Laying a path

All paths need a good foundation, and whether you decide on gravel or something more solid, the preparation is largely the same.

■ Dig a trench the width of the path, and the depth of the thickness of the surfacing material, plus 7.5cm for hardcore and 5cm for sand. For a gravel or concrete path the trench will not be as deep as you do not need the sand. The sides of the trench must be lined with shuttering boards if you are using concrete.

■ Ram the soil, then cover it with landscape membrane to prevent any deep rooted weeds coming through (this will not prevent weeds forming in the cracks later in but these will only be seedlings and can be easily removed or treated).

■ Add a 7.5cm layer of hardcore and consolidate again, then pour the concrete or top up with gravel.

■ Add the gravel or concrete, or, if you are using slabs or blocks, a 5cm layer of sand, well consolidated.If using concrete, remove the shuttering after a few days when the concrete is completely set.

■ Fill the cracks between the slabs with a dry mortar mix, or brush soft (builders') sand between blocks.

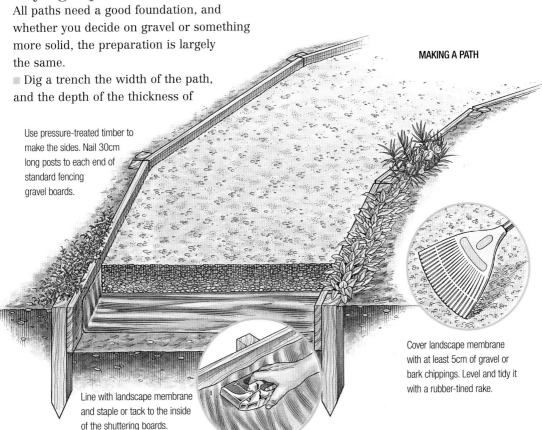

MAKING A PATH

Use pressure-treated timber to make the sides. Nail 30cm long posts to each end of standard fencing gravel boards.

Cover landscape membrane with at least 5cm of gravel or bark chippings. Level and tidy it with a rubber-tined rake.

Line with landscape membrane and staple or tack to the inside of the shuttering boards.

Techniques
for plants

AN OUTDOOR SEEDBED NEEDS CAREFUL PREPARATION. IT MUST BE FIRM, MOIST AND CONSIST OF A FINE TILTH. DIG HEAVY SOIL IN AUTUMN OR WINTER TO ALLOW IT TO SETTLE BEFORE THE FROST ARRIVES. LIGHT, SANDY SOILS CAN BE LEFT UNTIL SPRING. THERE IS NO NEED TO ADD ORGANIC MATTER; IF THE SOIL IS POOR, RAKE IN A BALANCED FERTILISER.

Plants that are sown outdoors:

The following flowers, vegetables and trees are all hardy enough to be sown straight into the ground.

- Brompton stocks
- Candytuft
- Canterbury bells
- Clarkia
- Godetia
- Hellebore
- Love-in-a-mist
- Nasturtium
- Sunflower
- Wallflower
- Beetroot
- Carrots
- Lettuce
- Parsnips
- Peas
- Spinach

- Oak
- Alder
- Norway spruce
- Silver birch

Hardy annuals are usually sown in March and April, but some can be sown in autumn to give the young plants a quick start in spring. Seed packets advise on the best times for sowing.

Perennials are treated in the same way as hardy annuals, but if you collect seeds from your own plants sow them as soon as possible. The viability of seed decreases with time, so sow old seed more thickly than fresh. Discard any seed that is more than two years old.

Pelleted seeds, coated with clay or other material, are easier to handle but need to be kept moist until the seedlings appear. Primed, also called pregerminated, seed is available for plants that need high germination temperatures.

Preparing the seedbed

1 In warm weather, when the soil is dry enough to walk on without sticking to your boots, hoe or lightly fork it over to a depth of 7.5cm. When the soil has dried out, tread it down firmly to break up lumps, then rake the surface to create a fine tilth (the particles should be small and evenly sized).

2 Prepare rows in the soil for sowing – running from north to south if possible so that the seedlings will receive the greatest amount of sunshine when they germinate. Space the rows according to the advice on the seed packet. Use the edge of a draw hoe (see page 20) to make shallow 'drills' about 1.5cm deep.

Sowing the seed

If the weather is dry, water the seedbed the day before sowing – not after sowing. Sow thinly to simplify thinning later. Or sow pinches of seeds at regular intervals according to the advice on the packet.

1 Mix very small seeds with fine sand to help to distribute them evenly. To control the seeds, dribble them from your hand between the folds in the skin.

2 To close the drills, use the back of a rake to pull the raised earth back over the seeds – working along the length of the rows, not across them.

3 Tamp soil down gently with the back of the rake. Be careful not to bury the seeds too deeply or to press the soil down too hard. As a rule of thumb, cover seeds with soil to about twice their size. Sow some surplus seeds at the end of rows so that you can use them to fill gaps later.

Thinning out the seedlings

Seedlings are ready to be thinned out when they have two or three 'true leaves', above the first pair of 'seed leaves'. If the weather is particularly dry, thin in the evening and water the bed afterwards.

1 Lift the unwanted seedlings from the soil with one hand while holding down the soil around nearby seedlings with the other. Remove weak or malformed seedlings first.

2 Thin the rest so they are spaced at half the distance required. Do not leave discarded seedlings on the ground; they will attract pests, so put them on the compost heap.

3 When the leaves of adjacent plants touch, remove alternate seedlings to leave the row at the full spacing. Fill any gaps with the surplus seedlings that were sown at the end of the rows.

PLANTS WHICH CANNOT SURVIVE IN THE OPEN DURING FROSTY WEATHER, SUCH AS HALF-HARDY ANNUALS, ARE FIRST SOWN IN CONTAINERS UNDER COVER – EITHER IN A GREENHOUSE OR INDOORS. THE TECHNIQUE CAN ALSO BE USED TO BRING ON EARLY BLOOMS OR CROPS.

Plants that are sown indoors:

These plants will do best if they are started off in a greenhouse or in the home.

- Begonia
- Bidens
- Cosmos
- Dahlia
- French marigold
- Busy lizzie
- Tobacco plant
- Pelargonium
- Petunia
- Scarlet sage
- Aubergine
- Basil
- Courgette
- Cucumber and gherkin
- Globe artichoke
- Pepper (sweet and chilli)
- Squash and gourd
- Tomatoes

Sow the seeds between February and early April. You can buy them from a garden centre or collect them from your own plants. Use plastic containers, as they are strong and easy to clean. Small seed trays or 13cm pots are usually most suitable. Scrub containers that have been used before in warm soapy water.

Sowing the seeds

1 Fill the container with slightly moist seed compost. When sowing very fine seeds, first sprinkle a little fine-sieved compost on the surface. Using the bottom of another pot, gently firm down the compost.

2 Sow seeds thinly and evenly. For easier control, fold the open flap to form a spout and carefully tap them out of the packet. Fine seed can be distributed more evenly if first mixed with a little silver sand.

3 Cover the seeds with a thin layer of sifted compost or vermiculite – a layer of about the seeds' own depth is enough. Some seeds should be left uncovered – very fine ones, such as begonias, lobelias and calceolarias, and those that need light to germinate, such as sinningias and streptocarpus.

4 Identify the contents with a plastic label. Stand the container in water to half its depth until the compost is wet.

5 Ideally, put the container in a heated frame or propagator at a temperature of 12-18°C. Or, cover the container with a polythene bag and fold it underneath. Stand it in a warm shady place, such as a shaded windowsill. For extra warmth put it in an airing cupboard, but check daily for germination and then immediately move it into the light.

6 Once seeds have germinated, turn the bag inside out each day to prevent drips. When growth is established, take off the cover and move into good light, but not direct sun.

Pricking out

1 Seedlings are ready to be 'pricked out' when the first true leaves appear above the seed leaves. Fill a standard seed tray – about 33 x 20cm – with moist potting compost and mark out plant holes about 4cm apart with a pointed stick or pencil.

2 Gently prise up a small clump of seedlings, complete with the compost clinging to their roots. Hold a seedling by a seed leaf – not the stem, which is easily damaged – and gently tease it from the other seedlings with the stick.

3 Lower the seedling into a hole and gently firm the soil down around it so that it will not yield if gently tugged. When the tray is full, label it and water the seedlings with a fine-rosed can.

4 Put the trays in a greenhouse or cold frame, or on a shaded windowsill. Three days later, move them to a sunnier, but lightly shaded, position. Keep the compost moist.

Hardening off half-hardy annuals

In early May, or April in mild areas, move the seedlings of half-hardy annuals outside but cover with an unshaded cold frame, cloche or polythene tunnel. For the first few days, open the frame or raise the sides of the tunnel slightly.

Gradually increase ventilation until – by mid May at the earliest (the end of May in northern England and frosty areas) – the coverings are completely open. You should delay opening the cloche, frame or tunnel fully if the weather is cold, wet or windy. Close all openings at night until the danger of frost has passed.

The danger of damping off

Seedlings planted too closely or overwatered may contract damping-off disease which causes rot at soil level. Remove and destroy dead seedlings or leaves and spray the rest with copper fungicide or Cheshunt compound. Next time, give your seedlings more space, and always use fresh compost and clean containers.

WHETHER YOUR NEW PLANT COMES IN A CONTAINER OR HAS BEEN PURCHASED WITH BARE ROOTS, USE THE CORRECT PLANTING TECHNIQUE TO GET IT OFF TO A HEALTHY START. CONTAINER-GROWN PLANTS ARE RAISED IN POTS OR TRAYS BUT HAVE WELL-DEVELOPED ROOT SYSTEMS; BARE-ROOTED SHRUBS ARE GROWN IN THE OPEN.

Dig over sites for new shrubs, trees and hedges well before planting if you can so that the ground has a month or two in which to settle. If you have no opportunity to prepare the whole area beforehand, you can plant immediately after digging individual sites.

Choosing a bare-root plant

■ Avoid plants with shrivelled or discoloured stems or buds that are beginning to grow or that have white hair-roots appearing.
■ Distorted stems may indicate a diseased or badly grown plant.
■ The soil around the roots of a rootballed plant is held together with netting.
■ To check condition, squeeze the rootball between your hands. It should be firm and moist. If the mesh is damaged or the soil too loosely packed, the roots may have started to dry out.

Preparing for planting

1 Mark out a circle, about 1-1.2m across, if you are planting in a lawn or grassed area.
2 Lift the turf and fork out any perennial weeds, then dig the area to the depth of a spade blade. Stack this topsoil to one side. Use a fork to loosen the subsoil and work in some garden compost or leaf-mould. Chop up any turf and lay this grass side down in the hole.
3 Prepare a planting mixture in the following way. Mix in a bucket 2.5l each of well-rotted manure and garden compost (or leaf-mould), plus 100g each of seaweed meal and bone meal, and fork this into the heap of excavated topsoil.

4 Before planting the tree or shrub add enough of the planting mix to raise the plant to the right depth.

Planting bare-root trees and shrubs

Bare-rooted trees and shrubs are ordered from a nursery in advance and delivered between November and March. They should be planted as soon as possible after delivery, but not when the ground is frozen.
1 Dig out a hole large enough to take the roots comfortably when spread out, and check the depth so the soil mark on the stem is at ground level. For trees, drive in a vertical stake 8-10cm off-centre and on

the lee side, away from the prevailing wind. Fork over the base of the hole and incorporate some organic matter such as garden compost.

2 Before planting the tree or shrub, soak the roots in water for 2 hours and trim off any broken or damaged roots. Hold the plant upright in position, spread a few trowels of planting mix (see 3, opposite) over the roots, and gently shake the plant up and down to settle the mix in place. Repeat and firm the plant lightly with your fist.

3 Half-fill the hole and gently tread firm. Check the plant is still at the correct depth and adjust if necessary by adding or removing soil.

4 Back-fill the hole, firm again and level the surface. Attach a tree to its support with an adjustable tie fixed near the top of the stake.

Planting a climbing shrub against a wall or fence

Climbers of borderline hardiness need a warm and sheltered spot, facing south or west. North and east-facing borders receive less sunshine and are exposed to the coldest winds. East-facing borders tend to be very dry because they are sheltered from the rain-bearing winds, which mostly come from the west.

■ The soil at the foot of a wall or fence is usually dry, so before planting dig in plenty of organic matter, such as garden compost, and give it a soaking. Make sure the soil is kept moist in future. Plant a climber 30cm away from the fence so it benefits from rain.

■ Ivy, Virginia creeper and climbing hydrangea fasten themselves to a fence and need no assistance once they have become established, but most other climbers need support throughout their lives. Put up trellis, horizontal wires or rigid plastic netting with a mesh size of 10-15cm. Fix it on battens 2.5cm away from the wall. Fasten shoots with string or a wire plant ring.

Planting clematis against a wall

1 Remove the pot and if the roots are spiralling around the rootball, tease them loose with your fingers.

2 Place the clematis in the hole, spreading out any loose roots, and position it so that the top of the rootball is 10cm below ground level. Then back-fill round the rootball, firm and water.

3 Spread out the plant's stems and tie them to several short bamboo canes, stuck into the soil at an angle to the wall. Do this for all climbers whether they are self-clinging or not.

64

How to transplant established shrubs

Shrubs – either deciduous or evergreen – can be moved
to a new part of the garden in autumn or spring, but not
when the soil is frozen or waterlogged. Small, young
shrubs transplant most easily.

1 Excavate a hole about 1m across and
45cm deep in the new site. Then use a
spade to mark a circle 60-75cm in
diameter around the plant to be moved.
Tie up arching branches with string.

2 Dig a trench one spade blade deep
outside the circle. With a fork loosen some
of the soil from the fibrous roots to reduce
the weight of the rootball.

3 Undercut the rootball by digging down
at an angle, slicing through woody roots.
Work round until the rootball is free.
Check that the new hole you have dug is
big enough, and adjust if necessary.

4 Tilt the plant to one side and ease a
piece of strong sacking or plastic sheet
underneath. Lean the plant the opposite
way and pull the sheet through.

5 Tie up the sheet securely to keep the
rootball intact, and lift or drag the plant
on the sheet to its new home. Plant at the
same depth as before, firm in, water well
and mulch.

Establishing a new container-grown plant

Container-grown shrubs are sold in plastic pots of compost. They can be planted at any time of the year, but if you plant them in summer make sure to keep the soil moist until autumn.

1 Remove all weeds from the bed, and dig over the soil to a spade's depth. Then firm the soil with your feet.

2 Dig a hole as deep as, and slightly wider than, the plant's container. The surface of the compost in the container should be level with the surrounding soil.

3 Break up the soil at the bottom of the hole with a fork or trowel and incorporate some organic material. Separately, mix some soil with more of the organic material.

4 Water the plant thoroughly. Then remove the container and check the extent of the root system (right). If the roots are wound around the outside of the rootball, gently tease out some of the outer roots so they will establish more quickly in the surrounding soil.

5 Holding the plant by the stem, and with one hand supporting the ball of soil, place it in the hole (below). Fill the hole to the top with the planting mixture and tread it down firmly. Top up with more of the mixture, tread down again and water thoroughly. Finally mulch the soil around the plant.

PLANTS COME IN ALL SHAPES, SIZES AND KINDS. CHOOSING THE RIGHT ONES NOT ONLY MAKES FOR A BEAUTIFUL AND THRIVING GARDEN, BUT WILL SAVE YOU TIME, MONEY AND DISAPPOINTMENT IN THE LONG RUN.

Plants for a purpose

Trees and shrubs

Woody plants are the back bone of any garden, whatever the size. They give height and form, and range from shrubs a few centimetres high to trees of several metres height and spread.

■ **Deciduous trees and shrubs** lose all their leaves in late autumn and produce new ones in the spring, while evergreen ones shed their oldest leaves a few at a time throughout the year, so are fully clothed year round. These include most conifers, which are trees and shrubs bearing cones.

■ **Evergreens**, particularly those with foliage other than green, are useful for giving colour in winter, but too many can make a garden look too much the same whatever the season. Many deciduous trees and shrubs have attractive bark or interesting branch structure, or have leaves that turn colour before they fall, and ones that have showy flowers, especially those that produce edible or ornamental fruit, including berries and nuts, are useful for seasonal interest.

■ **Roses** are also deciduous shrubs, but are such a big group that they form a category on their own, and this also applies to fruit trees and bushes.

■ **Most climbers** are shrubs that can climb through another woody plant or trellis by means of suckers, twining stems or tendrils. Some shrubs with a loose habit are trained as climbing or wall shrubs by pruning and tying in to a support.

The common beech (above) needs space but many weeping, columnar and coloured varieties are suitable for a smaller garden.
Prized for their delicate appearance, Japanese maples (below) are slow-growing and produce brilliant crimson autumn leaves.

Herbaceous plants

These are plants with non-woody stems. They provide flower, and sometimes foliage, interest at some period during the year. The two main groups are hardy and half-hardy perennials, which generally die down in winter and re-emerge in spring every year (although there are a few evergreen ones), and annuals and biennials, often known as bedding plants. These are planted for bold seasonal effect and are discarded at the end of their flowering period.

■ **True annuals** germinate, grow, flower, seed and die during the period of one year, but the term is sometimes used to describe perennials (petunias, for instance) planted for temporary effect.

The colourful trumpet-shaped flowers of petunias bloom from early summer until the first autumn frosts.

■ **True biennials** germinate and produce a non-flowering plant one year, then flower and die the next, but some biennials are actually perennials which have a short life or flower best in their first season (for example, wallflowers), so are treated as biennials.

■ **Bulbous plants** (those that produce shoots from underground fleshy organs known as bulbs, rhizomes, tubers or corms) are also herbaceous plants.

■ **Hardy plants** are those that will survive outdoors during a normal winter with no or minimal protection.

■ **Half-hardy plants**, including shrubs, annuals, perennials and bulbs, will not withstand frost and need to be over-wintered in a frost-free place, such as a well-insulated greenhouse or a cool, light room in the house.

■ **Tender plants** are those unsuitable for outdoor cultivation in the United Kingdom, and are usually grown for house or conservatory decoration.

Choosing the right plant

Always choose a plant that will not ultimately out-grow its space. This may mean your garden may look rather bare for a year or two, but you can always fill gaps with bedding plants if you do not like the look of bare earth.

When buying from a nursery or garden centre, avoid sick or spindly plants (even at bargain prices) and those with weeds and moss sprouting from the top of the pot, which is a sign of poor maintenance. Many roots emerging from the drainage holes at the base indicates that the plant should have been potted on some time ago, but if the compost looks loose and fluffy, it might be that it has just been repotted, and therefore needs to re-establish before planting out.

Clematis are available to bloom in every season, even winter. So with careful selection, you can enjoy their abundant blooms all year.

Mail-order plants are a much better buy than they used to be, but try to find out if the company is a stock-producing nursery, or just a business buying in from elsewhere, particularly from overseas, which can be less reliable.

Before accepting offers from friends, have a look at the parent plants – if they are taking over the garden, or are pest or disease-ridden, it is best to decline politely.

BEDDING PLANTS WILL BRIGHTEN UP EVEN THE DULLEST OF GARDENS, AND ARE INVALUABLE FOR NEAR-INSTANT COLOUR, OR A QUICK FIX WHILE YOU ARE DECIDING WHAT TO DO WITH YOUR PLOT ON A MORE PERMANENT BASIS.

If you have no time to raise your own bedding plants, they are readily available from nurseries and garden centres at the appropriate times of year, and the range of interesting varieties is widening every year.

Varieties of bedding plants

A bedding plant is a type of plant which is usually, though not always, raised indoors under glass either from seed or cuttings, and transplanted as a small, leafy specimen to the garden or container to produce flowers for temporary interest. There are two main types – those used for summer bedding, which are raised as half-hardy annuals and sown or raised from cuttings from late winter to mid spring for transplanting after risk of frost is past (usually mid May to early June depending on area), and those which are entirely hardy and raised from late spring to the end of June for planting in the autumn to give colour the following spring. Bedding plants are usually discarded at the end of their flowering season, though good specimens, especially of shrubby forms like fuchsias are sometimes kept as stock plants for cuttings. Bedding plants are usually chosen for their flowers, but others may be included for their foliage, like plectranthus, and a few (known as 'dot' plants) to give height to an otherwise flat bedding scheme – cannas are often used for this purpose.

Container planting

Until the rise in popularity of container gardening, bedding plants were always planted out in designated beds in the open ground, but are more popular now for tubs, troughs, window boxes and hanging baskets, or used to fill up gaps in mixed borders.

Traditionally, summer bedding plants comprise half-hardy annuals (such as *Salvia*

Planting bedding plants such as impatiens (far right) in containers is a good way to maintain a sumptuous display through the seasons.

patens), some hardy annuals (such as calendula), and some half-hardy perennials treated like half-hardy annuals (for example, petunias and pelargoniums). However, a few first year flowering hardy perennials have now been added to the list, and also many hardy plants with interesting foliage, such as *Glechoma variegata* (trailing nepeta), coleus, thyme, sage, lysimachia and ajuga (bugle). Spring bedding plants are nearly always hardy perennials raised as biennials – sown in spring and early summer of one year to flower and be discarded afterwards the next (for example, wallflowers, bellis, daisies, Brompton stocks, sweet williams, pansies and primroses).

Bedding plants for different seasons and situations

RELIABLE SUMMER BEDDING PLANTS

- Sweet alyssum
- Fibrous and tuberous rooted begonias
- Petunia
- Tagetes (French, African and Afro-French marigolds)
- Calendula (pot marigold)
- Lobelia
- Salvia patens
- Ageratum
- Impatiens
- Pelargonium
- Ten Week stock
- Antirrhinum

FOLIAGE BEDDING PLANTS

- Coleus
- *Plectranthus* 'Silver Shield'
- *Lysimachia nummularia* 'Aurea' (golden creeping Jenny)
- Senecio cineraria (Dusty miller)
- Ornamental kale (early winter)

SUMMER HANGING BASKET PLANTS

- Glechoma (trailing nepeta)
- Lotus
- Surfinia™ petunia
- Verbena
- *Pelargonium peltatum* (ivy-leaved pelargonium)
- Trailing fuchsias

'DOT' PLANTS

- Ricinus (castor-oil plant)
- Canna
- *Grevillea robusta* (silk oak)
- Standard fuchsias
- Kochia (burning bush, summer cypress)

SPRING BEDDING PLANTS

- Pansy
- Viola
- Forget-me-not
- Bellis (daisy)
- Primrose and polyanthus
- Brompton stock
- Sweet william
- Wallflower

Raising bedding plants

Most bedding plants are easily raised from seed, although summer ones require some warmth in spring for them to germinate. The alternative to this, and to buying plants ready to go out in their final positions, which can be expensive if you need a lot, is to buy plug plants. These are young ones raised in

Pretty violas are endlessly versatile. They are all good in rock gardens, at the front of borders and in containers.

Bearing crisp blooms in shades of orange and gold, marigolds have few rivals for ease of cultivation and length of flowering.

individual cells in trays, which are bought from the grower when old enough to withstand lower temperatures and are ready for potting on individually into larger plant pots or hanging baskets.

Bedding plants in the open ground should be kept well watered until established. Those in containers may need watering several times a day in hot, dry weather, and should never be allowed to dry out.

Hosta fortunei is one of the larger, sculptural hostas.

Herbaceous perennials are extremely versatile, and as well as making good border plants, can also be cultivated successfully in containers, especially those varieties that have attractive leaves.

Taller herbaceous perennials should be provided with stakes or metal supports as soon as growth starts in spring and tied in regularly as they increase in height. Avoid waiting until the plants flop over, or over-tightening the ties, as this makes for a bunched clump which is both unattractive to look at and can cause damage to the stems.

Cut back spent flower stems as soon as possible. This encourages new growth which may even produce a second crop of flowers, and removes untidy foliage to keep the overall appearance neat. However, some perennials, like solidago (golden rod), achillea (yarrow) and Aster novi-belgii (Michaelmas daisy) produce seeds that are attractive to many garden birds, and should be left if you enjoy watching them feed.

Herbaceous perennials for year-round interest

■ **Helleborus (Christmas rose, Lenten rose)** Flowers from Christmas until late spring, on evergreen or semi-evergreen plants of medium height. Prefers partial sun or light shade and moist soil. Propagate from division after flowering or seed. They make good container plants.

■ **Doronicum (leopard's bane)** Yellow, daisy flowers on 60-90cm stems from spring to early summer. Needs full sun or light shade. Tolerates most soil if not waterlogged. Propagate by division in autumn.

■ **Hosta (plantain lily)** Bold, mainly foliage perennials with broad, green, blue, cream, gold or variegated leaves emerging in spring and colouring well before dying back in autumn. White, mauve or lavender flowers in summer, some fragrant. Tolerant of sun or shade and dry or moist soil. Propagate by division in autumn.

■ **Heuchera (coral flower)** Showy evergreen, green, gold, orange, purple or bronze leaves, with dainty, bell-like flower spikes of green, white, pink, coral or red

Doronicum or leopard's bane makes a brilliant golden display.

produced from late May until autumn. Likes sun or partial shade and will cope with most types of soil. Divide large clumps in autumn.

■ **Primula** Includes primroses, polyanthus, auriculas drumstick and candelabra primulas, as well as the native cowslip. Flowers from spring to early summer. Rich, moist soil preferable. Propagate by seed in spring or division after flowering. Many primulas make good bog garden plants, and combine well with other moisture lovers, such as trollius (globe flower) and caltha (marsh marigold).

Dainty aquilegia (columbines), come in a wide range of colours and are easily grown.

■ **Geranium (crane's bill)** Not to be confused with the half-hardy pelargonium. Hardy geraniums flower from May to August, often with a repeat flush, and many varieties have evergreen leaves. They will tolerate most soils in full sun to half-shade, and can be propagated by seed or division.

■ **Aquilegia (columbine)** 'Granny's bonnet' flowers in May and June in a wide range of colours, on stems from 30-80cm according to variety. Full or partial sun and well-drained soil preferred. Propagate by seed or division in autumn or spring.

■ **Lupinus (lupin)** Spikes of peppery-scented flowers 90-120cm tall in a wide range of colours in June and July. Full sun and neutral or slightly acid, well-drained soil preferred. Propagate by seed.

■ **Delphinium** Range from 80cm to 2m or more, in a wide range of colours. Flower in June and July, and often again on shorter stems later in the season if cut back after flowering. Good soil and full sun preferable. Propagate from seed sown in spring or division in autumn or early spring.

■ **Helenium (sneezewort)** A daisy-like flower 60-100cm in height depending on variety that is very popular with bees, butterflies and beneficial insects. Likes full

sun and flowers from July to September. Many colours from clear yellow to deep red and bronze. Divide in autumn. Rudbeckia (cone flower) and echinacea (purple coneflower) will also attract beneficial insects to the garden.

■ **Sedum spectabile (ice plant)** The best plant for attracting butterflies into the garden in late summer and autumn, with flat plates of pink or reddish flowers and succulent light or greyish-green leaves. Needs a well-drained, sunny spot.

■ **Aster** Includes the Michaelmas daisy and other species with daisy flowerheads, such as Aster amellus, that attract butterflies and beneficial insects throughout summer and autumn. They need full sun and a well-drained (but not dry) soil and flower from July until October according to variety. Propagate by division in spring.

■ **Schizostylis (kaffir lily)** Flowers similar to gladiolus are produced from September until November. They need a sheltered, sunny place and can be propagated by dividing the rhizomes in spring.

The imposing spikes of lupins are a feature of early summer beds.

THE MOST LUXURIOUS OF FLOWERS WITH THEIR LAVISH BLOOMS AND HEADY FRAGRANCE, THERE IS A ROSE FOR ALMOST EVERY SITUATION, FROM TINY PATIO ROSES TO ROMANTIC CLIMBERS AND RAMBLERS TO FESTOON A DOORWAY OR RANGE OVER A FENCE, CLASSIC GLAMOROUS BUSH ROSES AND LOW-GROWING SPECIES FOR PRETTY GROUND COVER.

Site and soil

Most roses need plenty of sun – preferably for at least three-quarters of the day. Avoid shady and exposed windy sites. Slightly acid soil, with a pH of 6.5, is best. A medium loam retains the water they need but does not become waterlogged. Improve light soils by adding as much humus-forming matter as possible. Mulch regularly to suppress weeds and cut evaporation. Apply a layer about 7.5cm thick in late spring when the soil has begun to warm up and a powdered or granular rose fertiliser twice a year. Scatter a handful round each plant in spring, and again soon after mid summer, when the first flush of bloom is over.

Planting roses

Before planting, cut out any damaged or diseased shoots from the top growth and trim back tough roots by a third. Make the planting hole wide enough for the roots to spread out and deep enough for the budding union to be 2.5cm below the soil surface. Work a small handful of rose fertiliser into

A scrambling rose in a brilliant colour will add grace and glamour to even the humblest surroundings.

the soil at the bottom of the hole, then set the plant in the hole. Work in soil round the roots so that there are no air pockets, then fill in the hole and tread soil down firmly.

Training climbing roses

■ When growing a rose on a wall, tie the shoots to wires threaded through vine eyes driven into the brickwork and stretched horizontally about 45cm apart up the wall.
■ When training a rose up a pillar, spiral it round the support.
■ When training into trees, use a large, strong tree in prime condition. Train the rose towards the tree along a stout cane or rope tied at an angle between the trunk and a long peg driven into the ground.

Rose hedges

Many shrub roses make excellent hedges. Train spreading shrub roses along horizontal wires strung between posts or on a chain-link fence. Rugosas and upright shrub roses rarely need such training.

Deadheading

The removal of spent blooms (deadheading) induces a repeat-flowering rose to try to produce more hips and seeds, allowing it to produce a second flush later in the season. Deadhead at least twice a season, after each main flush or when you see a faded flower by snipping off the spent flower. Do not deadhead species roses or any other roses grown for their decorative hips.

Recommended roses

Bush roses

■ **Intrigue** (cluster flowered/floribunda)
Deep crimson, semidouble flowered, opening to show golden stamens.

■ **Golden Showers** Golden-yellow, upright, branching habit, medium height. Good for training up pillars.
■ **Compassion** Salmon-pink, HT shaped flowers all summer, very fragrant. Strong, healthy growth.
■ **Antique** Rose-pink with pale pink centres, cabbage rose-shaped blooms. Vigorous, disease resistant.
■ **Madame Alfred Carrière** White flowers from pale pink buds. Fragrant. Easily trained. Tolerates a north-facing position.

Rambling roses
■ **Alberic Barbier** Yellow buds opening creamy-white, double and fragrant. Almost evergreen foliage.
■ **Albertine** Copper, fading to salmon-pink, scented, profuse.
■ **New Dawn** Shell-pink, fragrant, repeat flowering. Strong, healthy growth.

Shrub roses
■ **Rosa xanthina 'Canarybird'** Very early, single, yellow, fragrant flowers. Tall, arching.
■ **Hybrid musk 'Buff Beauty'** Masses of apricot-yellow flowers, heavily scented. Long flowering season. Medium height.
■ **'Ballerina'** Bushy, huge heads of small, single, pale pink flowers with white eye.
■ **'Nevada'** Semidouble, fragrant, white flowers in May and June, second flush in August to summer's end, Sturdy habit to 2m.
■ **'Graham Thomas'** New English rose with yellow, fragrant flowers all the season. Strong growth, medium-tall habit.
■ **Rosa moyesii 'Geranium'** Red flowers followed by flagon-shaped hips. Compact.

Ground-cover roses
■ **Essex** Pink, repeat flowering. Bushy.
■ **Partridge** Wide spreading, white, single or semidouble flowers.
■ **Red Blanket** Rose-red, semidouble heads, perpetual flowering. Fairly prostrate.
■ **Flower Carpet series** Pink, coral, red, yellow and white on low-spreading bushes.

■ **Royal William** (large flowered/hybrid tea) Crimson, fragrant, strong growing; tallish.
■ **Sea Pearl** (CF/F1) Pear-pink, suffused peach and yellow. Free flowering.
■ **Silver Jubilee** (LF/HT) Salmon-pink, shaded peach. Fresh fragrance, disease resistant.
■ **Arthur Bell** (CF/F1) Large, golden-yellow flowers, fragrant with glossy, leathery leaves.
■ **Peer Gynt** (LF/HT) Yellow, shaded orange. Compact, bushy habit.
■ **Just Joey** (LF/HT) Coppery-orange, veined red, pales to apricot towards edge of petals.
■ **Hannah Gordon** (CF/F1) White, shading to cherry-pink. Deep bronze-green foliage.

Miniature and patio roses
■ **Orange Sunblaze** Orange red.
■ **Gentle Touch** Pink, tall miniature.
■ **Top Marks** Orange vermilion patio rose. Abundance of blooms.
■ **Sweet Dream** Orange-yellow to apricot.
■ **City Lights** Deep yellow, very fragrant

Climbing roses
■ **Danse du Feu** Orange-red, medium grower. Tolerates shade; can be grown on north wall.

SHRUBS ARE THE BACKBONE OF THE GARDEN, PROVIDING FOLIAGE AND FLOWER COLOUR IN SUMMER, FORM IN WINTER, WHILE EVERGREENS KEEP THE INTEREST ALIVE IN WINTER. NO GARDEN IS TOO SMALL FOR AT LEAST ONE OR TWO, AND PRACTICALLY EVERY SHRUB CAN BE GROWN IN A CONTAINER, FOR A FEW YEARS AT LEAST.

Shrubs may be grown in a bed or border on their own, and a shrubbery is an ideal feature if time for maintenance is limited, as weeds are easily hoed off or treated with a herbicide, and there is little other regular maintenance. Many shrubs can be planted in a lawn or gravel, or suitable varieties can be planted slightly closer than normal along a boundary to make an unusual, informal hedge. Adding shrubs to an herbaceous border will give height and structure, especially in winter, when most of the other plants have all but disappeared.

Flowering shrubs give a boost to the garden when in bloom, but can look rather dull when not in flower, so where space is limited, choose ones that have additional attributes, such as variegated foliage and combine them with interesting evergreens or those with coloured bark. Find out before you buy how tall and wide-spreading a shrub will get after, say, five or ten years. If it is likely to outgrow its space, look for a more restrained variety. It is impossible to cut back a flowering shrub to make it smaller as you will cut off all the potential flowering shoots. A shrub grown for foliage can be kept smaller by regular cutting back.

Looking after shrubs

An established shrub will not, in general, need regular pruning, but if some reduction or rejuvenation is required, it is best done immediately after flowering if it flowers up to the middle of August, and in spring for late-flowering varieties; evergreens are pruned in spring or late summer. The best way to keep a shrub young and healthy is to remove about a third of the oldest branches completely after flowering; new shoots will appear from the base and after three years it will have a brand new branch framework.

Try to include a few shrubs to attract wildlife into the garden. These include *Buddleja, sambucus* (ornamental elder), cotoneaster, *ilex* (holly), *ribes* (flowering currant), and *Viburnum opulus* (guelder rose). All shrubs, even when quite small, make possible nesting habitat for birds in summer and roosting sites in winter.

Cornus alba

Shrubs for modern gardens

- **Aucuba japonica 'Variegata' (spotted laurel)** A variegated evergreen that will survive almost anywhere, sun or shade, wet or dry, and in any soil. Female plants produce berries if planted with a male.
- **Berberis darwinii** Medium-sized evergreen with small, bright green, spiny leaves and red tinted new shoots. Produces golden-yellow flowers in late spring and early summer, followed by black berries. Sun or light shade, normal soil.
- **Buddleja davidii (butterfly bush)** Attracts butterflies when in flower. Semi-pendulous spikes can be white, blue, lavender and purple. Prefers full sun and dry, slightly poor soil. Propagate by seed, or hardwood cuttings in autumn. Cut back hard in spring.
- **Choisya ternata 'Sundance' (golden Mexican orange blossom)** Small evergreen shrub with nutmeg fragranced leaves and masses of fragrant, white flowers in late

spring and early summer. Full sun, most soils. Propagate from summer cuttings.

■ **Cornus alba (red-stemmed dogwood)** An evergreen shrub with brilliant autumn colour. Sun or shade, moist soil. White flowers in late spring, then white berries, turning blue, then black. Propagate from hardwood cuttings in autumn. Cut hard back every two years for best bark colour.

■ **Elaeagnus pungens 'Maculata' (oleaster)** Variegated evergreen leaves, responds well to regular cutting back. Small, very fragrant flowers in autumn and early winter. Tolerant of most conditions. Take cuttings in summer.

■ **Forsythia** Spring-flowering shrub, easily propagated from cuttings in summer or autumn. Various sizes and variegated forms obtainable. Sun or partial shade, any soil.

■ **Hebe** Large genus of evergreen flowering shrubs, ranging from a few centimetres to about 2m. Grow in full sun on well-drained soil. Take cuttings in summer.

■ **Hypericum (St John's wort)** Small or medium sized semi-evergreen shrub. Showy, yellow flowers most of the summer. Most positions and soil conditions. Propagation by summer cuttings or seed.

■ **Philadelphus coronarius 'Variegatus'** Medium-sized, variegated mock orange, with perfumed, creamy-white flowers in June.

Purple lilac

Full sun and good, fertile soil. Propagate by semi-ripe cuttings in late summer.

■ **Ribes sanguineum (flowering currant)** A small to medium sized shrub, flowering very early in spring, attracts early bees and other insects. Flowers deep red to white, then blue-black 'currants'. Can be pruned fairly hard just after flowering to keep neat. Propagates easily from hardwood cuttings in autumn, or seed over-wintered outdoors.

■ **Skimmia** Small shrub with dark green, evergreen leaves. Fragrant spring flowers. Neutral or slightly acid, moist soil and light shade. Propagate by cuttings in summer.

■ **Syringa (lilac)** Sun or light shade and most soils. Can be pruned hard after flowering without affecting flowers later on. Lilacs growing on own roots can be propagated by suckers in autumn.

■ **Viburnum tinus** Medium to large evergreen shrub with blush white flowerheads in late winter and spring. Tolerates most conditions. Propagate by removing new shoots from around the base in early spring, or by layering at any time of year.

■ **Weigela florida 'Variegata'** A small shrub as attractive in leaf as in flower, with pale yellow and green foliage sometimes tinged pink and red and tubular, pink flowers in June. Most sites except dense, dry shade or waterlogged soil. Propagate from cuttings taken in the second half of summer.

Forsythia blossoms

THERE IS A TREE FOR NEARLY EVERY GARDEN. WHERE SPACE IS TIGHT, GROWING A SMALL OR SLOW-GROWING TREE IN A LARGE TUB WILL RESTRICT GROWTH ENOUGH TO MAKE IT MANAGEABLE, BUT CHOOSE THE TREE TO SUIT YOUR SITE; NOTHING LOOKS WORSE THAN A LARGE ONE THAT HAS BEEN CHOPPED BACK BECAUSE IT HAS OUTGROWN ITS SPACE.

In spring and early summer ornamental trees come into their own, with flowers of every colour and size. If you only have room for one or two, trees with attractive fruit extend the season of interest, and those with leaves that change colour during spring and autumn also work in a compact plot.

When adding trees to your garden, remember that those in the nursery or garden centre are only young, and will alter light, moisture and other factors as they grow. Find out the height and spread in five, ten and 20 years before you buy so you don't have to remove it later because it has made the area too shady or too dry, cut out a favourite view, or smothered other plants.

A newly planted tree usually needs support to prevent wind rock. Secure the trunk to a stout stake with tree ties that will expand as the tree grows. Or use two stakes set a little way apart with a horizontal piece of wood between them near the top, to which the tree is tied, or a sloping stake driven well into the ground at an angle – the young tree is secured firmly to this where the trunk and the stake meet. Make sure that the tree does not rub against the stake or it may suffer serious, permanent damage.

Trees for modern gardens

■ **Acer x conspicuum 'Silver Ghost'** A 'snake bark' maple with striking bark and leaves that colour well in autumn.
■ **Acer pseudoplatanus 'Brilliantissimum'** A small to medium sized sycamore with leaves opening shrimp pink, turning yellow and finally green in summer.
■ **Acer x Betula utilis 'Silver Shadow'** A lovely birch with brilliant white young wood and bark, suitable for a modest garden.
■ **Catalpa bignonioides 'Aurea'** Yellow-leaved form of the Indian bean tree, with very large, velvety leaves and pendulous racemes of white, foxglove-like flowers on mature plants, followed by pods.
■ **Cercis canadensis 'Forest Pansy'** Has pink flowers along the branches in May as the beautiful, reddish-pink foliage unfolds. Slow and suitable for a small garden.
■ **Fagus sylvatica 'Dawyck Gold'** A narrow, columnar beech tree with bright gold leaves. 'Dawyck Purple' has deep copper purple leaves. Suits a medium garden.
■ **Gleditsia triacanthos 'Sunburst'** Golden yellow, small to medium with ferny foliage. For a small garden, the slow-growing *Gleditsia triacanthos* 'Ruby Lace' is better.
■ **Magnolia 'Susan'** A medium sized magnolia with an upright habit and large, reddish-purple flowers in profusion in spring.
■ **Malus 'Rudolph'** Leaves open bronze-red, and turn green, with bright, rosy red flowers and orange-yellow fruit.
■ **Prunus 'Royal Burgundy'** Medium sized with double pink blossom in spring and large, deep burgundy coloured foliage.
■ **Prunus 'Okame Harlequin'** Small tree with pale pink flowers in early spring, and small leaves variegated green, cream and pink throughout summer.
■ **Salix purpurea 'Pendula'** Narrow, with graceful, thin, pendulous branches, purple bark and long grey-blue leaves. Slender catkins occur all along the branches.
■ **Sorbus aucuparia 'Sheerwater Seedling'** Mountain ash with close, upright habit, heads of white flowers in May, and orange-red berries from late summer. Leaves turn fiery red, orange and yellow before falling.
■ **Sorbus aria 'Lutescens'** Medium sized with a rounded head. Silver leaves on purple shoots in spring turn green with grey below. Clusters of white flowers in spring, followed by red berries like small cherries.

CONIFERS HAVE A PLACE IN EVERY GARDEN, HOWEVER SMALL, AS THERE ARE TREES RANGING IN HEIGHT AND SPREAD FROM MANY METRES TALL, WHICH ARE ONLY SUITABLE FOR THE LARGEST AREAS, TO JUST A FEW CENTIMETRES, MAKING THEM IDEAL FOR ROCK GARDENS, CONTAINERS AND SMALL BEDS.

Conifers come in foliage colours from green and blue to gold and pale cream, and many different shapes to add form to every design. They do not look the same year-round, as new spring shoots can be quite different in colour, and many varieties turn red or bronze in winter. Most are evergreen, but *Ginkgo biloba*, the maidenhair tree, and *larix* (larch) lose their leaves after turning bright yellow in autumn.

Most conifers prefer well-drained but moist soil, but some, like *Taxodium distichum*, the swamp cypress, like their roots in boggy ground. If your garden is dry, you will find that junipers will cope better than most. Conifers associate well with heathers, and, in the case of dwarf forms, alpines and rock garden plants, but can be planted together to form a bed comprised entirely of conifers, or added to the mixed or shrub border for extra interest.

When buying conifers, do your research first, as size in the nursery is no indication of final height and spread. A small plant may grow to be a giant, while large specimens of dwarf varieties can create instant effect.

A range of conifers

■ **Abies koreana** A slow-growing, medium sized fir tree with dark green needles, white underneath, and showy, cylindrical cones.

■ **Cedrus deodara** A large cedar tree with pendulous branches and bright green needles. Makes good specimen plant for a large lawn, but grows very large in time.

■ **Chamaecyparis lawsoniana 'Summer Snow'** A small to medium conifer with feathery foliage and white new shoots, turning cream then pale green.

■ **Cryptomeria japonica 'Elegans'** A medium to large conifer with feathery foliage turning bronze-red in winter. A good specimen for a large shrubbery or lawn.

■ **Juniperus horizontalis 'Emerald Spreader'** A completely prostrate, wide-spreading conifer which is ideal for ground cover and bank planting.

■ **Juniperus scopulorum 'Skyrocket'** The complete opposite of 'Emerald Spreader', this juniper makes an extremely narrow, blue-grey column and is good for accent planting, but also looks great grouped in threes in a conifer bed.

■ **Picea abies 'Pygmaea'** A tiny, very slow-growing form of Christmas tree, suitable for a small rockery or sink garden.

■ **Pinus mugo** Also known as the mountain pine, this is a medium sized pine with a dense, bushy form and comparatively long needles. It is very lime tolerant, so will thrive in chalky soils.

■ **Taxus baccata 'Standishii** A slow-growing, golden yew with an upright habit. It is useful for 'dot' planting, but can be used as a slow-growing, easy-maintenance hedge.

Conifers come in such a wide range of forms, shapes and sizes that there should be one to suit almost every garden.

TRUE CLIMBERS ARE PLANTS WHICH ARE CAPABLE OF SUPPORTING THEMSELVES ON A STRUCTURE BY MEANS OF TENDRILS, SUCKERS, OR TWINING LEAVES OR STEMS. IN ADDITION, YOU WILL OFTEN FIND LISTED AS CLIMBERS, PLANTS WITH A SPREADING OR WEAK-STEMMED HABIT THAT CAN EASILY BE TIED IN AND PRUNED TO COVER A SUPPORT.

Climbers are useful for adding a 3-D effect. In a tight space, they give the opportunity to grow a plant in limited space, especially with roses. They can be used to cover a trellis, pergola, arch, wall or fence. Twining and tendril-producing forms are most suitable for an open-work structure, while lax, or wall shrubs, are better for training on a trellis, wall or fence using wires. Climbers that cling to their supports with suckers, such as ivy and Virginia creeper are best on a wall, but tend to leave suckers behind when they are pulled off; as these are difficult to remove, so think very carefully before planting. They do not damage surfaces or kill trees, but may smother young tree growths.

Wisteria will form a graceful arch to embellish architectural features or walls.

Always choose the right climber for the aspect on which it is to grow. Many clematis, will burn up in the hot sun of a south or west-facing wall, but will thrive and produce brighter coloured flowers in shade, while a hot wall is just the place for a sun lover like campsis, solanum or actinidia.

Recommended climbers

- **Actinidia kolomikta** Grown mainly for its green, pink and white leaves, but mature plants have white, fragrant flowers in June.
- **Campsis radicans (trumpet vine)** Self clinging with red or yellow trumpet-shaped flowers. Needs warmth and fertile soil.
- **Ceanothus dentatus** Evergreen shrub often trained against a wall, where it often produces more and better flowers.
- **Clematis** Huge family with great variety and spread, and flowers almost all year round according to variety.

- **Cotoneaster horizontalis** Self-supporting if placed close to a wall. Masses of pink buds, open white in early summer followed by red berries.
- **Hedera (ivy)** Many varieties with small, medium and large, often variegated leaves and slow to rampant habit. Mature plants produce clusters of greenish flowers and blue-black berries.
- **Hydrangea petiolaris (climbing hydrangea)** A self-clinging climber with flat plates of white flowers in early summer.
- **Jasminum (jasmine)** *Jasminium nudiflorum* is a winter-flowering shrub. Others flower in summer and need full sun for best results. Many are scented.

Lonicera (honeysuckle) A twining climber with attractive, mostly fragrant flowers.

Parthenocissus tricuspidata (Virginia creeper) Planted for its showy green leaves with spectacular autumn colour. Self clinging; young plants may need support.

- **Passiflora (passion flower)** Choose *P. caerulea* for outdoor cultivation in a warm, sunny site. Orange fruits may form in some seasons, but these are unpalatable.
- **Pyracantha (firethorn)** Easy to train as a wall plant. White flowers in early summer followed by red, orange or yellow berries.
- **Solanum (perennial nightshade, climbing potato)** Sprawling climber with showy flowers of white or purple, and sometimes red berries, throughout summer and autumn. Needs a warm, sheltered place.
- **Wisteria** Late spring/early summer climber with long racemes of white, pink, purple or blue flowers. Choose a named cultivar as seedlings may flower poorly.

Buying bulbs

Try to plant bulbs as soon as possible after delivery. Erythroniums, trilliums and other bulbs without a skin or 'tunic' should be kept in moist bark or compost. The best flowers come from the biggest bulbs, so choose the largest you can afford. The 'second-size' bulbs are more economical for naturalising in large quantities. With loose and pre-packed bulbs look for clean, firm and plump examples, with no obvious root or shoot growth. Avoid those that are dirty, soft, damaged, shrivelled, or showing signs of mould or pale, forced shoots and roots. Be wary of bulbs kept in warm conditions, as they are more likely to be soft and actively growing than those in a cool, dry atmosphere.

Planting bulbs

Ideally, you should finish planting daffodil bulbs by the end of August, as their roots start growing in late summer. But there is usually no harm in waiting until September, the usual time for planting other spring-flowering bulbs (except for tulips). If you are planning a bedding display with wallflowers and other spring-flowering plants, you can even wait until early October in mild areas.

■ **Bulbs in borders** look more appealing flowering in informal groups. Before planting, enrich a light soil with plenty of garden compost or well-rotted manure. Or, if your soil is heavy, dig in some coarse sand or grit to improve drainage.

■ **Smaller bulbs**, such as fritillaries, snowdrops or crocuses, add charming informality to areas of a lawn or wild garden, especially under deciduous trees.

■ **Before planting in grass** mow the area as short as possible. Remember that after flowering you must wait at least six weeks before mowing the grass, to allow the bulb foliage to die down naturally and ensure flowers in future years.

Planting bulbs in the border

1 Dig out a large planting hole wide enough for the bulbs to be at least their own width apart and deep enough so they are covered with soil to two or three times their height.

2 Scatter a little bone meal over the base of the hole and lightly fork in, then water gently before positioning the bulbs.

3 Gently cover bulbs with soil, making sure you don't knock them over, then tamp the surface firm with the back of a rake and label the area.

1

2

3

4

Naturalising bulbs in grass

1 Cut the outline of a large 'H' through the turf using a spade. This makes it easier to under-cut the turf from the middle and peel back two panels to expose a rectangle of soil. Loosen the soil underneath with a fork.

2 Fork in bone meal at a rate of 15g per m². Then scatter the bulbs over the exposed soil and press each one in gently; they should be at least 2–3cm apart.

3 Make sure the bulbs are upright before carefully replacing the turf.

4 Firm the turf gently with your hand and, if necessary, fill the joints with fine soil.

Lifting and storing corms in winter

In areas where the weather is mild, gladioli, ixias and sparaxis corms may be left in the ground throughout the year. Elsewhere, when the leaves begin to brown in October, the corms should be lifted.

1 Carefully lift the corms with a fork. Cut off the top stems and leaves to within about 2.5cm of the corm. Place the corms in trays

1

Deadheading

Deadhead outdoor bulbs by pinching off large heads such as daffodils and stripping off the faded flowers of hycinths but leave the stalks and leaves intact to die down naturally.

and leave uncovered for seven to ten days in a cool airy shed to dry.

2 Break away old shrivelled corms and put aside any small cormlets for increasing stock. Remove the tough outer skins from the large corms and burn any that appear to have lesions or that are rotting.

■ Dust the corms with pirimiphos-methyl to control thrips. To prevent dry rot and gladiolus scab, dust with sulphur or dip in a solution of carbendazim. Store in trays in a cool but frost-free place until spring.

LATE SPRING, WHEN THE SOIL IS WARM AND MOIST, IS THE IDEAL TIME FOR A NEW LAWN TO ESTABLISH RAPIDLY. GRASS GROWS BEST FROM TURF OR SEED IN MOIST BUT WELL-DRAINED SOIL, AND GOOD LIGHT IS USUALLY ESSENTIAL, ALTHOUGH LAWN MIXTURES THAT TOLERATE SOME SHADE ARE AVAILABLE.

Planning your lawn

The size and shape of the lawn depends on the size and style of your garden: sweeping curves suit an informal setting; straight lines are more formal. If you are planning narrow strips of grass, make these multiples of the cutting width of your mower. This will make mowing easier and give a more even finish.

Whether grown from turf or seed, make a new lawn slightly larger than its ultimate planned size. This allows you to trim back the edges once the lawn is established to give a crisp outline.

Seed or turf?

Before creating a new lawn, the big decision is whether to lay turf or sow seed. Turf provides an instant effect, but it is much more expensive; seed is cheaper, but takes longer to establish. The deciding factor tends to be how long you are prepared to wait.

Lawn seed mixtures

■ **Fine ornamental lawns** These lawns look lush and beautiful, but will not stand up to hard wear. Mow with a cylinder mower for a fine close finish, and one with a roller for stripes.
Sowing rate: 35-50g per m²
Mowing height: 1-1.5cm
■ **Lightly shaded lawns** This is the best mix for lightly or partially shaded areas where the soil is moist, but unsuitable for deep shade, dry soils or under evergreen trees.
Sowing rate: 35-50g per m²
Mowing height: 1.5-2cm
■ **Hard-wearing lawns** This mix produces a tough, good-looking lawn, tolerant of heavy use and children's games throughout summer.
Sowing rate: 25-35g per m²
Mowing height: 1.5-2cm

Preparing the ground

A lawn is a permanent garden feature, so it is worth preparing the ground thoroughly to avoid future problems. Deep and thorough digging is particularly important to ensure that the soil is well cultivated where most root activity occurs, and grass roots penetrate surprisingly deeply. First of all remove all traces of perennial weeds. Use a spade to dig the area to a depth of at least 25cm. Carefully remove all weed roots and creeping stems. You can do this by hand as you dig, but where the ground contains a high proportion of perennial weeds, such as horsetail, you may need to use a chemical weedkiller based on glyphosate to eradicate weeds from the soil completely.

Sowing seed

A seeded lawn may be slow to establish but, when sown at the optimum times in spring or autumn, the result is usually of a good quality. You can also select a seed mixture that suits your garden situation. Most reputable seed mixtures are a blend of two or more species of grass that will grow well together and provide an even, dense coverage. The species of grasses usually differ in their mode of growth and at least one will have a creeping habit. The sowing rate will vary depending on the seed mixture and the intended use for the lawn, so check the instructions on the packet.

SOWING TIP Sow at a slightly higher rate than recommended to achieve a thicker-looking lawn in a shorter period of time.

Sowing a lawn

1 After digging thoroughly, use a garden fork to break up any compacted soil to improve drainage. Level the soil, then allow it to settle for about two weeks. Any emerging weeds can be hoed off or treated with a systemic weedkiller based on the chemical glyphosate.
2 Rake the soil roughly level. Incorporate a base dressing of fertiliser applied at the rate of 150–200g per m².
3 Firm the soil by shuffling over the ground applying pressure with your heels. Rake the soil again and remove any stones.
4 To sow the seed evenly, mark out the area into 1m squares with canes and a string line. Weigh out enough seed for 1m². Pour the seed into a plastic beaker and mark the level on the side. Use this measure to save weighing the seed every time.
5 For each square, sow half the seed in one direction and the remainder at right angles.

Pour a manageable quantity into your hand at a time and scatter evenly.
6 When you have sown all the seed, lightly rake the entire area to incorporate the seed into the soil surface. Water well.

Lawns from turf

Laying turf is the gardener's equivalent of carpet laying and the job must be done just as carefully and as systematically for a good result. So first prepare the soil as described on page 81 and mark out the area slightly larger than required.

Turf may be expensive, but about six weeks from being laid, the lawn should be well established and ready for use. This method is not without its drawbacks during the early stages. Newly laid turf needs to be kept well watered, and in warm dry weather this could mean as much as 25l per m² each week. If turf is allowed to dry out it will shrink and lift, exposing a much greater surface and accelerating the drying process; whereas if there is a spell of dry weather immediately after grass seed has been sown to make a new lawn, the seeds will simply remain dormant until the conditions for germination improve, rather than beginning to grow immediately.

Turfing a lawn

1 Starting from one corner, lay the first row of turf alongside a plank or garden line to get a straight edge. For lawns with curved edges, lay a hosepipe or length of rope to define the boundaries.

2 Go back to the starting point to lay the second row of turfs at right angles to the first. This ensures that the joints are staggered, like bricks in a wall; it is called 'keying' the turfs together. As you work, butt the turfs up close to each other.

3 Work from a wooden plank; this protects the turfs from damage caused by walking on them as subsequent rows are laid. The uniform pressure will also gently firm the turfs into position after they are laid, helping the grass to establish.

4 When all the turfs are down, spread a lawn top dressing (available from garden centres) over the entire area and brush it into any gaps or cracks with a besom broom or the back of a rake. This helps to stop the turf edges from drying out and shrinking.

Buying turf

Turfs are usually sold in sections 1m x 30cm and rolled along their length. Many of the more expensive turfs are reinforced with a biodegradable plastic mesh, so less soil is needed to hold the root structure together and the turfs can be thinner and up to 2m in length. For extensive lawns it is possible to buy turf as a large roll, which is laid out by a contractor and cut to the exact dimensions, like a fitted carpet.

Mowing new lawns

New lawns sown from seed early the previous autumn or in April will be ready for their first cut at the end of May, but only a very light topping is required for the first two or three cuts. If you use a rotary mower, sharpen the blades well beforehand so that they will cut the grass rather than drag it out by the roots. Rotary mowers rely on the speed of the blades to get a cutting action,

but a combination of blunt blades and shallow-rooted grass seedlings can wreak total havoc on a newly establishing lawn.

Whichever type of mower you have, use one with a roller if possible, as the pressure of the roller will bend over the young blades of grass, thus checking their rate of growth. The plants respond by branching from the base to produce many more leaves, which thickens the coverage of the lawn considerably. Some gardeners even roll a new lawn two or three times before the first cut to encourage this branching growth (called 'tillering'). Checking the top growth and stimulating extra root development produces an established lawn more quickly.

The first three or four cuts of a new lawn should be made on a high blade setting. As the grass starts to thicken, you can gradually lower the height of the cut, but no more than a third of the total height should ever be removed in a single cut.

Watering new lawns

Freshly laid turf dries out very quickly if not kept moist, and lawns raised from seed will also dry out rapidly because the grass leaves do not yet cover the soil surface sufficiently to stop it from drying out. With turf, immediately after laying the turfs, brush a 'top dressing' of loam and sand into the joints to help to reduce drying out and therefore shrinkage.

Water all newly made lawns for at least 2-3 hours every three or five days if there is no significant rainfall. The best way to do this is to leave a seep hose running at a gentle trickle on the lawn, moving it every half hour.

Aerator

Scarifier

Fertiliser spreader

Lawn rake

Feeding lawns

Regular mowing gradually saps the strength of the grass. If nutrients taken up by grass and removed as clippings are not replaced, the lawn loses its vigour and is vulnerable to disease. To overcome this problem, feed the grass as soon as growth starts in spring.

All spring lawn feeds contain high levels of nitrogen to promote rapid, green leaf growth. If you are using fertiliser in powder or granular form, water it in if no rain falls within 48 hours of its application.

Apply solutions of lawn feed through a hose dilutor. For small lawns, use a watering can and dilute the solution according to the manufacturer's instructions on the label.

Lawn health

To stay green and healthy, grass needs more attention than simply mowing. Remove moss and dead grass debris and fallen leaves and aerate your lawn.

■ **Aerator** This introduces air into the soil and aerates roots. It consists of a frame of tines or blades. These are pushed into the ground all over the lawn. Those with hollow tines remove tiny cores of soil that can be replaced with a top dressing or sand.

■ **Scarifier** Removes surface debris and dead grass. It is pushed over the lawn, rotating a series of tines or blades that rake through the grass.

■ **Fertiliser spreader** A drum on wheels that is pushed along, while rotating blades below the drum spray out the granular fertiliser for up to 1m on either side.

■ **Lawn rake** With spring tines arranged in a fan shape, this tool is ideal for raking out moss, leaves and removing surface debris.

Lawn equipment

■ **Shears** With straight handles set as an extension of the cutting blades, garden shears cut like scissors. They are useful for grass where the mower cannot reach. Edging shears have long handles set at right angles to the cutting blades and are used from a standing position to trim grass growing over the lawn edge.

■ **Half-moon edger** With a curved metal blade mounted onto a spade shaft and handle, the half-moon edging tool is used to trim lawn edges and cut turf.

FRUIT TREES AND BUSHES CAN BE AS REWARDING AS ANY ORNAMENTAL PLANT.
TREES TRACE DECORATIVE SHAPES AGAINST A SUNNY WALL – AS WELL AS GIVING FRUIT.
AND STRAWBERRIES, RASPBERRIES AND CURRANTS PROVIDE DELICIOUS SUMMER TASTES.

Fruit crops require less work in spring than vegetables and, once established, they require little attention and will bear rich rewards for many years. You can reduce maintenance time by choosing easy-care fruit and by growing them in the correct situation (see illustration, below). The best site to grow most fruit is one that gets sun for at least half the day, but is sheltered, with well-drained soil that retains moisture in summer. To save time, position fruit crops where they will be easy to water and prune. Some of the more decorative fruit trees can be incorporated into the ornamental part of the garden.

Choosing where to plant

An apple tree makes a good focal point in a lawn. Choose a half-standard with a 1.2m trunk; a bush tree with a trunk about half this length; or a 'Ballerina' tree, which forms a natural column without pruning and casts little shade. After planting and staking, lay a sheet mulch (available ready-cut in 45cm or 90cm squares). Disguise black plastic with bark chippings, but wool-mix sheets look

WHERE TO GROW FRUIT
Choose the right type of fruit for the situation. Use the illustration below to help you to decide where to plant fruit in your garden.

In a fruit cage This is the best place to grow soft fruit because it provides protection from birds and shelter from the wind. In a small cage, grow fruit that will benefit most from the protection – redcurrants, strawberries, raspberries and even a dwarf cherry tree.

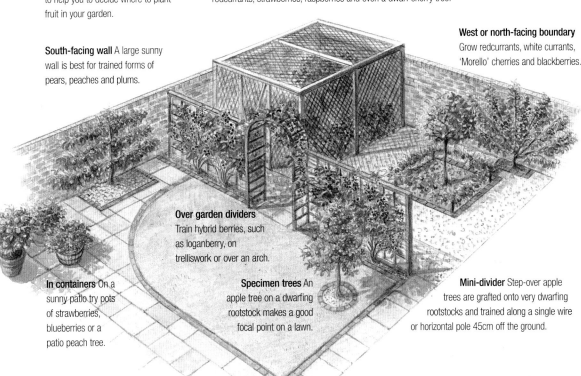

South-facing wall A large sunny wall is best for trained forms of pears, peaches and plums.

West or north-facing boundary Grow redcurrants, white currants, 'Morello' cherries and blackberries.

Over garden dividers Train hybrid berries, such as loganberry, on trelliswork or over an arch.

In containers On a sunny patio try pots of strawberries, blueberries or a patio peach tree.

Specimen trees An apple tree on a dwarfing rootstock makes a good focal point on a lawn.

Mini-divider Step-over apple trees are grafted onto very dwarfing rootstocks and trained along a single wire or horizontal pole 45cm off the ground.

acceptable as they are. A sheet mulch will prevent weeds from competing with the young fruit tree for moisture and nutrients, so less time needs to be spent on improving the soil (see page 33).

■ **Sunny fences or walls** are an ideal site for trained fruit, such as plums or pears and hybrid berries. Although training involves a little extra work and skill, the benefits include an attractive cover to the fence with two seasons of interest. By training the tree you will make picking the fruit easier. Cordon apple or pear trees can be a productive alternative to a conventional screen or barrier in a garden. You will need full access on at least one side for pruning and tying in new growth to supporting wires.

The easiest fruit to grow

Tree fruit

■ **Apples, raspberries, redcurrants and strawberries** are easy to cultivate, as well as being useful in the kitchen. Apples are the easiest tree fruits to grow because they are

Keeping fruit trees small

Fruit trees are available in a range of different rootstocks. The rootstock determines the vigour of the tree and how big it will grow. If the rootstock is not stated on the label, don't buy the tree.

Fruit	Rootstock	Size of tree
Apple	M27	1.2-1.8m
	M9	2.5-3m
	M26	3-4.5m
Pear	'Quince C'	3-3.5m
Cherry	'Colt'	3-5.4m
Plum	'Pixy'	1.8-2.5m
	'St Julien A'	3-5.4m

hardy and suitable for most soils – even neglected trees produce some crops. The size of the mature tree is determined by the particular rootstock (see above). You need two or three different varieties to cross-pollinate each other. To save having to grow more than one tree, check that there are other suitable apple or ornamental crab

In a larger garden, you may be able to sustain a number of apple trees. They also look gorgeous laden with blossom in spring.

The development of smaller varieties has made it possible for cherry trees to be netted against birds when the fruit is ripening.

apple trees in neighbouring gardens. Alternatively, choose a 'family tree' which has different varieties grafted onto the same rootstock. Late-flowering varieties are less likely to suffer from frost, which damages flowers and prevents pollination. Some varieties, such as 'Charles Ross' and 'James Grieve', can be used both as cooking and dessert apples.

■ **Pears** are less hardy and less tolerant of wind than apple trees and need more shelter and warmth. However, they can be trained as single-stemmed cordons against a warm wall. Pears will also need another compatible variety nearby to pollinate the flowers.

■ **Plums** blossom early so they are prone to frost damage. Varieties of plums that are fan-trained are easier to protect from frost because you will be able to use netting. Choose self-fertile varieties, such as 'Victoria' and 'Czar', so that only one tree needs to be grown.

■ The fruit of **large-growing cherries** is often devoured by birds before harvesting. Trees on dwarfing rootstocks are easier to grow and to protect with netting. 'Morello' cherries are the only tree fruit that will grow in the shade, including a north-facing wall. However, they are suitable only for cooking. A few varieties of cherry are self-fertile, including 'Stella', so they do not need another variety to act as a pollinator.

Bush and soft fruit

Check out specialist fruit catalogues for varieties of soft fruit offering disease resistance. New varieties are being introduced each year.

■ **Blackberries** are too vigorous for most gardens, although unlike most other fruit they tolerate wind and shade. Hybrid berries, such as the thornless loganberry, are tasty and pretty in flower. They can be trained against a sunny fence.

■ **Blackcurrants** are easy to grow, though fiddly to pick. The fruit is of limited use fresh, but makes excellent jam and desserts. Redcurrants are sweeter than blackcurrants. They are easy to grow, but protection from birds is essential. Cordon-trained plants produce the heaviest crops, and are the easiest to pick, prune and protect from raiding birds.

■ **Gooseberries** are spiny, so picking and pruning can be unpleasant. Vertical cordons produce larger fruit which is easier to pick. Like currants, they need to be shaded from hot summer sun. Thin fruit in early summer and use the small, unripe fruit for cooking, leaving the rest to mature on the plant. The plants are long-lived.

Although not suitable for a smaller garden, vigorous blackberries are useful if you have more challenging conditions as they will thrive in both exposed and shady spots.

Versatile strawberries can be grown in a small garden and will do well in a container, growing bag or even a hanging basket.

■ **Raspberries** are easy to pick and very versatile, whether used fresh or frozen. Summer-fruiting types are usually grown in a line with a wire support. After fruiting, the old canes are cut out and the new canes tied in. The easiest to grow are the autumn-fruiting varieties such as 'Autumn Bliss'. They need no supports and are simply cut down to ground level in February.

■ **Strawberries** crop a few months after planting, making them a popular choice of fruit. They grow best planted through a mulch of black polythene in mounds of raised earth. Use cloches or netting to protect them from birds. Plant new stock every two to four years on a new site. Alpine strawberries make pretty, easy plants for shaded areas of the garden. The fruits are small and tasty but not juicy.

Preventing pests and diseases

A lot of problems can be avoided by keeping the garden tidy and taking action before they start. For instance, by picking up windfalls and diseased leaves in autumn, you can prevent fungal spores from overwintering on them. A garden vacuum will save time. In October or November, attach grease bands, available from garden centres, to the trunks of apple trees to prevent female moths climbing up to lay their eggs. Place the bands 60cm from the ground and check them regularly to make sure they are in good condition and that the barrier is not breeched by leaves or other debris. Leave them in place till April. Also put up pheromone traps (see right) in late spring to catch the male codling moths.

When crops are growing, be vigilant for signs of attack. Use the chart opposite to identify serious problems and take remedial action immediately. When checking crops, remove and destroy foliage with grey mould, eggs or aphids (greenfly) on them, and pick off any caterpillars that you see. Preventive spray programmes are not worth while because they have to be applied at such precise times with so many precautions that it is rarely practical, except perhaps on the

Easy-care fruit

■ Choose varieties that are naturally resistant to diseases.

■ Provide the best possible site and growing conditions.

■ Keep weeds under control – maintain a 90cm diameter weed-free zone around young fruit trees, and a 45-50cm wide strip on either side of cane fruit.

■ Don't choose complicated, trained forms – they take longer to prune.

■ Don't allow fruit to go short of water, particularly when swelling.

Aphids suck the sap from plant leaves and distort plant growth. They excrete a sticky honeydew on which sooty moulds develop.

Pests and diseases to look out for

Few pest and disease outbreaks on fruit are worth worrying about. However, the following can severely damage the crop or weaken the plants and so action is necessary.

■ Blackberries and hybrid berries
Can be spoilt by raspberry beetle grubs in fruit. Control with contact insecticide after flowering.

■ Currants
Big bud mite They cause swollen buds on blackcurrants, eventually weakening bushes. Pick off stems showing symptoms.

Aphids Pucker leaves and weaken the plant. Use contact insecticide.

Coral spot This appears as small red spots on stems. It particularly affects redcurrants, and should be pruned out.

■ Apples
Codling moth Tunnelling larvae damage fruit making them unusable. Prevent damage by hanging up pheromone traps in late spring. These trap male codling moths. One trap will protect up to five trees.

Scab It is a waste of time storing apples with scab (brown patches on fruit and leaves). There is no effective control, so prune out affected twigs and prevent future outbreaks by clearing away windfalls and fallen leaves in autumn.

Powdery mildew This affects young shoots and leaves, which should be removed and destroyed.

Canker Causes sunken patches on branches. Cut out affected wood when seen.

■ Raspberries
Many pests and diseases attack raspberries, but if plants still produce edible fruit simply cut out affected canes.

Raspberry beetle Maggots found in the fruit – but 'Autumn Bliss' is rarely affected. Control with contact insecticide after flowering.

■ Gooseberries
Mildew A common and serious problem. Spray with a systemic fungicide. Replace plants with a resistant variety such as 'Invicta' or 'Greenfinch'.

Sawfly Caterpillars eat leaves and can defoliate whole stems during late spring. Pick off any caterpillars you see or use a contact insecticide.

■ Strawberries
Grey mould Affects fruit in wet summers or when the plants are watered from overhead. Pick off mouldy fruit when you see it and clear away dead leaves.

Slugs Apply pellets to prevent slug damage.

smallest trees. For the busy gardener, a low level of pests and diseases should be considered acceptable on fruit, especially tree fruit. Also, by not spraying, you can enjoy pesticide-free produce.

If pests do become a problem, prompt action will save time and effort in the long run. For instance, aphids must be controlled because they spread rapidly, weakening plants by sucking their sap and spreading viruses. Options include winter washor summer spraying. In early summer, a soap-based spray or an aphid control based on pirimicarb can be used if aphids are visible. Some raspberry varieties are resistant to raspberry aphid.

Serious diseases, such as honey fungus, fireblight or red core (which affects

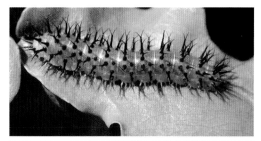

Sawfly larvae (above) burrow through the cores of apples and plums while greedy slugs (below) eat the leaves of many plants.

strawberries in particular) are best dealt with by removing and destroying the plants, and then starting again on a fresh site. To avoid the risk of root disease when replanting fruit trees or bushes, do not plant on a site where previous crops grew.

Other diseases that attack the woody framework of the plant can be fatal, too. Canker on apple or pear trees needs to be pruned out. Red spots on the wood are a sign of coral spot, which can spread onto live wood and should therefore be cut out immediately.

Over the years, soft fruit can be progressively weakened by viruses, so replace plants when their yields become low. Buy fresh, healthy stock rather than propagating your own – not only is this quicker, with less risk of viruses, but you have the opportunity to try out newer disease-resistant varieties.

Buying and growing fruit plants

Garden centres and seed catalogues sell a limited range of fruit, but the biggest selection of newer varieties and disease-resistant varieties are available from fruit specialists. Orders are taken in autumn and winter and plants are dispatched during the dormant season – from November to March. Strawberries are the exception: they should be bought container-grown in summer (runners are cheaper, but harder to establish). Buy virus-free plants and avoid any with foliage that has yellow mottling or streaks. Many types of soft fruit are sold 'certified' as being pest and disease free. This guarantee is worth paying extra for.

Planting

Bare-root specimens should be planted straight away in order to prevent the roots from drying out. Otherwise, put them in a shallow trench with the roots covered until you get a chance to plant them properly. Container-grown specimens can be planted at any time of the year, but for the least work do it in autumn, when the ground is naturally moist. Avoid planting during dry spells. Before the fruit is planted, the ground should be free of perennial weeds.

Aftercare

A thick organic mulch of well-rotted manure, garden compost or bark chippings is essential. Top up the mulch once a year in spring. At the same time, apply a general-purpose, balanced fertiliser, such as blood, fish and bone, Growmore or a rose fertiliser. For fruit trees, apply fertiliser over an area just beyond the spread of the branches. Do not apply fertiliser to strawberries unless grown in a container. Give plants extra water when the fruit is swelling.

Harvesting

Most fruit needs harvesting in summer, and dry evenings are a good time. Pick the fruit carefully, especially if you want to store it. Use shallow containers, such as seed trays, to prevent crushing soft fruit that is needed whole. Leave apples and pears on the trees as late as possible. Pick early apple varieties

Allow apples to ripen on the tree and pick them when they detach easily from their stalks. Don't allow them to over-ripen; it will affect the number of flowers produced next year. On a free-standing tree, ripening starts on the south side which receives the most sun.

from August onwards and use straight away because they don't store well. Leave late varieties until early to mid October and harvest before bad weather damages them or blows them to the ground.

Storing fruit

■ **Storing dry** Good-quality apples are worth storing. Don't store bruised or holed fruit or windfalls. There is no need to wrap apples singly, simply put them in polythene bags with a few holes in and tie the bag loosely. These can then be kept in the garage or other cool, dry place for six to eight weeks. Check them regularly and remove any deteriorating fruits.

■ **Freezing** Raspberries and prepared apples freeze well, as do currants and gooseberries.

■ **Preserving** Blackcurrant jam and redcurrant jelly are a delicious way of storing fruit. Freeze the currants until you have time to make preserves.

Easy pruning of fruit trees

Established apple and pear trees benefit from light pruning each winter. Dwarf trees are the easiest to reach to prune. There is no need to prune cherries and plums; make sure you buy trees that are already trained to a good shape.

Awkward branches Prune out any upright branches that are difficult to pick and that shadow other branches.

New growth Shorten about half the new sideshoots to maintain the tree's overall shape.

Dead wood Remove any diseased or dead wood, cutting back to just above a bud.

Overcrowded branches Remove crossing and overcrowded branches to make the tree less congested.

Pruning cordon trees

Cordons, espaliers and fans of apple or pear trees are trained in the same way. Treat each branch of espaliers and fans as single cordons.

In summer Prune new sideshoots along the main stem back to three buds beyond the rosette of leaves at the base.

In winter Cut back the tip of the main stem to a convenient height (around 1.8m) to keep the tree easy to reach for picking.

Pruning fruit bushes and canes

Cane fruit are simple to prune. Easiest of all are autumn-fruiting raspberries, which can be cut back to ground level in February. New shoots will then grow in spring and fruit in autumn. For summer-fruiting raspberries, see right. Blackcurrants are the easiest bush fruit to prune.

Other established bush fruit, such as gooseberries and redcurrants, need pruning in both summer and winter (see below).

Summer-fruiting raspberries Cut old canes that have fruited right back to the ground either after harvesting or by autumn. Select strong new canes and tie them in 10 cm apart. Remove all others.

Gooseberry and redcurrant bushes In winter (right), cut back the leaders by half their length and remove any dead, diseased or damaged wood.

In mid summer (above), prune back the new sideshoots to about 10cm, but leave the leading shoots.

Gooseberry and redcurrant cordons After mid summer, prune sideshoots to 10cm from main trunk. In winter, shorten the leader by a third.

EATING YOUR OWN HOME-GROWN FRUIT, VEGETABLES AND HERBS IS SUCH A PLEASURE THAT EVEN A VERY BUSY GARDENER MIGHT BE TEMPTED TO TRY GROWING A FEW FOOD PLANTS. YOU CAN KEEP WORK TO A MINIMUM BY PLANTING TROUBLE-FREE VARIETIES AND USING MODERN TECHNIQUES.

All crops, especially salad leaves, potatoes and strawberries, are so much tastier when eaten freshly picked from the garden that you may decide that it is time well spent. New and improved varieties, and labour-saving techniques and products, such as growing under crop covers and using automatic watering systems, help to make home-grown produce a realistic option even if time is at a premium.

Herbs, tomatoes and salad crops are the best plants for the novice vegetable gardener to start with because they are highly productive and can be grown in small spaces. Success on a limited scale may inspire you to extend your range of crops, or even to tackle a whole vegetable plot or a fruit garden. Fruit trees and bushes are a particularly good investment because, once established, they will produce crops year after year. Annual applications of well-rotted organic matter to the soil reduce the need to water.

Planning for success

Good planning is the key to growing fruit and vegetables successfully when time is short. Work out how many hours you can spend each week tending your plot, then concentrate your efforts on crops that will give maximum rewards for the time you have. Try to spread the workload throughout the year by completing non-seasonal tasks during the winter months.

You don't need a large garden or even a dedicated area of the garden to grow your own produce. Some crops, especially herbs, salad vegetables and strawberries, can be raised in containers. If you want to grow just a few plants, then start with a pot or two on a patio. It is not only easy to do, but you get quick results because no ground preparation

Make the most of your crops

- Grow only the crops you know that you and your family want to eat.
- Plan ahead: work out how much time you can spend each week before deciding what to grow.
- Draw up a cropping plan of what you will grow during which season and where.
- Choose pest and disease-resistant varieties where they are available.
- Invest in fruit cages and crop covers to protect your produce.
- Concentrate on growing fewer crops well.
- Don't grow too much of one thing or it will go to waste.
- Don't bother with crops that are difficult to grow or that are unreliable performers.

or weeding is required. However, once you have more than half-a-dozen containers, the time spent planting, watering and feeding mounts up and would be more productively spent on looking after crops planted in the ground.

Some food crops make attractive additions to the flower border. Chives or strawberries, for instance, make an easy-care edible edging, while fruit trees can be trained to grow against a wall or fence alongside a flowering clematis or rose, or used as a productive garden divider. Cropping will be reduced, however, if plants have to compete with others for light, moisture and nutrients.

A plot dedicated to fruit and vegetables avoids problems of competition and is easier to protect from pests and diseases. You can take a lot of hard work out of growing vegetables by using a raised, no-dig bed with paths in between (see page 95).

A vegetable bed can be a decorative feature as well as a practical one. For

Scented arch Sweet peas smother this west-facing arbour that catches the evening sun.

Fruit crops Apple and pear trees are planted against the wall, standard gooseberries add height to the square beds and step-over apples form a garden divider.

Central herb bed The clipped bay tree makes an attractive focal point, surrounded by easy-care herbs.

A GARDEN TO PROVIDE A FAMILY'S FRUIT AND VEGETABLES The formal layout makes for a decorative potager at the sunniest end of the garden, near the house.

Adding height Climbing vegetables, including runner beans, climbing french beans, trained courgettes and squashes are supported on wigwams of bamboo canes.

example, geometric beds containing vegetables can be combined with archways covered by runner beans or perhaps a trained courgette plant. Many vegetables are surprisingly attractive plants. For colourful leaves, try beetroot, red cabbage and red 'leaf lettuce'; ruby chard has brilliant red stems. You can make the productive plot blend in with the rest of the garden by growing flowers for cutting, such as chrysanthemums and dahlias. Sweet rocket, nasturtium, pot marigold, viola and pansy, all have edible flowers that are ideal for adding to salads or cold summer drinks.

The rewards of growing vegetables

As well as the benefit of fresh, tasty and interesting produce without the need to visit the supermarket, many busy people also find vegetable gardening an enjoyable way to exercise and relax. A productive plot can be easily maintained as long as you follow a few time-saving golden rules. The first is to grow only what you and your family like to eat and in appropriate quantities. Consider when it will need to be harvested and make sure that this will fit in with the other parts of your life. For instance, if you go away every August, grow vegetables that crop before and after then. Above all, make good use of your time by growing a few vegetables well rather than many badly.

■ **Digging** This chore can be almost eliminated by separating the walking areas from the growing areas using a no-dig bed system (see right). Create a series of beds with paths in between for easy access. Add a raised edge, such as gravel boards made of pressure-treated softwood, to help to prevent the beds spilling onto the paths. Once the no-dig bed is built, apply a thick mulch of well-rotted organic matter each autumn, letting earthworms incorporate it into the ground for you over winter. Although deep beds take longer to construct and prepare, they will repay the effort with time saved over the long run.

■ **Watering** Reduce the need for watering by applying a mulch in early spring to keep moisture in the ground. Water only those crops that will benefit most (see 'When to water', page 96). Apply the water to the rooting area, doing the job thoroughly every week – or consider investing in an automatic watering system.

■ **Weeding** For quick results, destroy perennial weeds when preparing a plot with a glyphosate-based weedkiller. For a seedbed, after preparing the ground, cover it with clear polythene to warm the soil and to encourage weed seeds to germinate. Hoe off the weed seedlings before sowing the vegetables: hoe shallowly so that you don't bring a fresh crop of weed seeds to the surface. Concentrate on hoeing around young vegetables before their leaves start to touch between the rows. The crops will then create so much shade that no further weeds will germinate. Hoe on a regular basis so

MAKING A NO-DIG BED FOR VEGETABLES

The easiest way to grow vegetables is in a raised bed with paths in between. The soil doesn't become compacted because it is never walked on – so eliminating the need to dig. The deep bed allows for closer spacing and, combined with regular mulching, reduces the need for weeding and watering. Make each bed 1-1.5m wide so you can reach with ease into the centre of the bed from the path.

Finishing off

Make the path Lay down a sheet of water-permeable membrane to prevent weeds. You can disguise the sheeting with gravel or bark chippings. Tend the plants from the paths and do not walk on the bed.

Protection Use wire hoops to support crop covers (polythene or insect-proof mesh) or buy a cage which is ready-made.

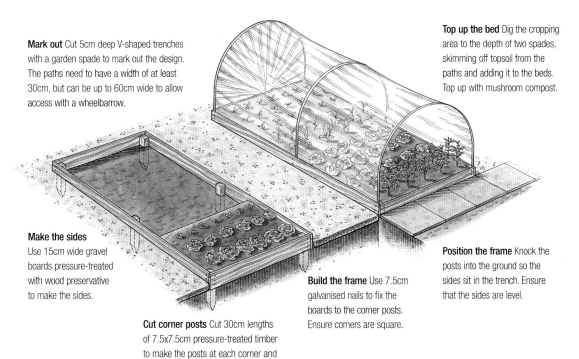

Mark out Cut 5cm deep V-shaped trenches with a garden spade to mark out the design. The paths need to have a width of at least 30cm, but can be up to 60cm wide to allow access with a wheelbarrow.

Top up the bed Dig the cropping area to the depth of two spades, skimming off topsoil from the paths and adding it to the beds. Top up with mushroom compost.

Make the sides Use 15cm wide gravel boards pressure-treated with wood preservative to make the sides.

Build the frame Use 7.5cm galvanised nails to fix the boards to the corner posts. Ensure corners are square.

Position the frame Knock the posts into the ground so the sides sit in the trench. Ensure that the sides are level.

Cut corner posts Cut 30cm lengths of 7.5x7.5cm pressure-treated timber to make the posts at each corner and at the centre of the longest sides.

that weeds do not develop beyond tiny seedlings; they can then be left to shrivel up and die on the soil surface and you won't have to clear them up. Hoe on dry, sunny days only because many weeds will reroot in damp soil.

Easy-to-grow vegetables

Most vegetables are annuals so they need sowing or planting afresh each year. Hardy vegetables are easier to start off than tender types, which need frost protection. But tender plants, such as courgettes and runner beans, are easy once frosts have passed provided you grow only a few plants. Vegetables vary as to how fussy they are about soil conditions and the amount of attention they need. You will get better yields from those that can more or less fend for themselves (see 'Vegetable selector', on page 98).

To spread your workload during the garden's busiest time – in spring and summer – create two beds, one for hardy crops and the other for frost-tender ones. Prepare and plant the one for hardy vegetables in March or April and the other at the end of May. You will then be able to stagger the work of soil preparation and planting. Only the bed for hardy crops needs to be weeded and watered between March and the end of May, while the other is kept covered with black polythene in order to stop weed growth. This method will also give you a good spread of vegetable types.

Overwintered onions are an easy winter crop to grow. Plant them as sets in mid autumn; by late spring you can start pulling the biggest, then harvest the rest by early summer. With some crops, such as runner beans and courgettes, you will need just a couple of plants to get lots of produce, but you will need to pick them over regularly in summer. When following a recipe, easy-to-grow vegetables can substitute difficult ones; leaf beet, for example, is easier to grow than spinach, and leeks and spring onions can replace onions because they are less fussy about soil and less likely to run to seed, or 'bolt'.

Since the choice of vegetable varieties changes rapidly, the table on page 98 indicates what features to look for in order to help you to choose the best from the seed catalogues.

Vegetables in containers

If you do not have space for a vegetable bed you can grow a few crops successfully in containers. Pots will need regular watering and liquid feeding (use a balanced feed for leaf crops, a tomato feed for fruiting crops). They need to be at least 20cm deep and to have drainage holes. Start with easy crops, such as runner beans, early potatoes, carrots, tomatoes, spring onions and salads.

Perennial vegetables

A few vegetables are perennials so once planted they will produce crops year after year. The following are worth trying.

■ **Asparagus** Once established, a bed will last 10 to 20 years. Asparagus needs a well-

Runner beans Use a large pot and keep well watered. Choose the variety 'Pickwick'.

Tomatoes Choose a trailing variety such as 'Tumbler' for a hanging basket. Plant after the last frosts have passed. Spray plants against blight in mid summer.

Spring onions Pull 12 to 14 weeks after sowing as required. Choose the variety 'White Lisbon'.

Potatoes Use an early variety, such as 'Rocket', in a container at least 30 cm deep and wide. Plant sprouted tubers in late spring.

Carrots Use a short variety, such as 'Suko', for growing bags. Pull when 5-7.5cm long.

Salad crops Loose-leaf lettuce can be grown in containers 15 cm deep. A window box or trough is an ideal size.

drained site. Plant 30-45cm apart. Plants are easier than crowns or seed. Choose an all-male hybrid, such as 'Franklin', that can be cut in its second year.

■ **Rhubarb** Can crop for five to ten years or so. Needs rich, well-drained soil. Plant a virus-free division in winter in soil enriched with organic matter. Mulch each spring. Remove flowering stems. Try 'Timperley Early', good for forcing, or 'Victoria'.

■ **Jerusalem artichokes** Tolerant of rough ground and heavy soil. Plant tubers in spring. Plants will need supports because they grow to 3m high. Cut off flowerheads. Cut back stalks in autumn. Try 'Fuseau' for ease of cleaning.

■ **Sorrel** Ideal for partial shade. The leaves have a sharp lemon flavour and can be picked through winter in mild areas if cloched. Pick outer leaves first, leaving middle leaves to grow. Remove seed heads. Plants are very hardy and last for three or four years.

Growing healthy crops

Taking early steps to prevent pests and diseases will save a lot of time in the long run. Always keep your vegetable-growing area clear of rubbish and remove dead plant material immediately – put it on the compost heap or, if it is diseased, put it in the dustbin or burn it.

Always buy healthy plants – potatoes, in particular, should be certified virus-free, so check before you buy. Vigorous plants are less likely to succumb to pests and diseases than weak ones, so aim to build up a fertile soil that is rich in organic matter.

Crop covers in modern materials were developed for commercial growers and can be a boon to the busy gardener. There are two types of crop cover: garden fleece and insect-proof mesh.

■ **Garden fleece** is laid loosely over newly planted tender plants to protect them from unseasonal frosts and flying pests, while allowing water through. Leave the fleece on for about four weeks after planting, then remove once the weather gets warmer. Clean it at the end of the season by putting it in a washing machine.

■ **Insect-proof mesh** is a more durable netting that is better ventilated than fleece so it can be left on all summer, but it does not provide any frost protection. Plants can be watered through the covers so remove them only when the plot needs weeding or the plants pollinating.

You can also help to prevent pest problems by taking a leaf out of the organic gardener's book and enlisting the natural enemies of plant pests. Aphids, for example, are eaten by birds and ladybirds, while slugs are eaten by frogs. Encourage these beneficial creatures to forage in your garden by providing a suitable habitat.

As soon as you see any pests, eggs or any diseased leaves, remove them by hand. If a serious pest or disease outbreak occurs, apply a ready-to-use spray to save time diluting and mixing concentrated chemicals. Remove plants that are suffering from viruses – shown by their yellow-streaked, mottled or spotty leaves – since there is no cure and the virus can easily spread to and damage other plants.

Vegetable selector

Many vegetables are easy to grow – an ideal choice for the busy gardener. Others need some help to establish but are worth the effort.

Vegetable	Easy to grow	Worth the effort	Keeps well in the soil	Features to look for when choosing a variety
BEETROOT	✓		✓	Bolt resistant (e.g. 'Boltardy')
BEAN, BROAD	✓		✓	Short ones need less support
BEAN, FRENCH	✓			Dwarf ones need less support
BEAN, RUNNER	✓			Reliable (c.g.'Desiree', 'Polestar')
CALABRESE		✓		Easier than cauliflower or broccoli and more productive
CARROT	✓		✓	Early varieties grow faster than main crop
COURGETTE		✓		Compact types take up less room, but give same crop
GARLIC	✓			Any variety
LEAF BEET		✓		Easier to grow than spinach
LEEK		✓	✓	Reliable (e.g. 'Musselburgh')
LETTUCE		✓		Bolt resistant
ONION, SPRING	✓			Reliable (e.g.'White Lisbon')
PEA	✓			Mangetout easy to prepare
POTATO		✓		Early ones (e.g. 'Maris Bard')
RADISH	✓			Any variety
RUBY/SWISS CHARD		✓	✓	Easier to grow than spinach
TOMATO, OUTDOOR		✓		Bush or trailing types

Dealing with pests and diseases

■ **Clubroot** A fungal disease of brassicas which deforms and rots the roots. Spores can remain in the soil for many years. Remove and burn affected roots. In future, lime the soil to pH 7.5 and start brassicas in pots before planting out. Try resistant varieties.

■ **Slugs/snails** Large holes in leaves and other plant tissues. Use slug pellets after planting.

■ **Aphids (greenfly)** Weaken plant and can spread viruses. Spray plant (including underside of leaves) with pirimicarb or dimethoate. Pull up and dispose of plants with root aphids. Control black-bean aphid by pinching out growing tips of broad beans after four flower trusses have set.

■ **Eelworms** Serious soil pests with few control methods. Move your vegetable plot to a different part of the garden or grow in containers.

■ **Birds** Pigeons can attack brassicas and take pea and bean seeds. Net crops in early spring.

■ **Beetles/weevils** Telltale signs are small holes in young leaves or nibbled leaf edges. Dust brassica seedlings with derris. Next year use a crop cover for protection.

■ **Mice** They can eat pea and bean seeds. Raise plants in pots and plant out once established.

■ **Root pests** Cabbage root fly eat roots of brassicas, lettuce and root crops. Work soil insecticide into the top 5cm of soil before planting. Use brassica collars.

■ **Root flies** Affect carrots, cabbages and onions. Flies lay eggs at soil level; these hatch into small grubs which attack the roots. Use a crop cover to stop flies laying eggs next year.

■ **Rust** Causes orange spots on leek foliage. Remove diseased leaves. There is no cure.

■ **Root rots** Widespread leaf discoloration or wilting is often the first symptom. Remove and destroy affected plants. Improve soil conditions.

■ **Caterpillars** Butterflies and moths lay eggs on the underside of leaves. Pick off by hand; spray or use a biological control (*Bacillus thuringiensis*). Use a crop cover to prevent the problem reoccurring.

■ **Blight** Attacks potatoes and tomatoes. Cut off top growth from affected plants to limit the spread. Spray in early summer with copper-based fungicide in wet periods.

■ **Downy mildew** Causes the yellowing of brassica and lettuce leaves, and makes the tips of onion foliage die back. Remove affected specimens, thin the remaining plants and spray with mancozeb.

CROP ROTATION

If the same crop is grown on the same soil year after year, pest and disease problems will build up. If you grow a wide range of vegetables, it pays to plan a crop rotation. Make feeding and soil improvement easier by grouping vegetables of the same family. In the three-year rotation (year one shown below), cabbage family crops are grown on soil previously used by the pea family to take advantage of the legumes' ability to 'fix' nitrogen in the soil. Grow salad crops in between slower-growing crops anywhere on the plot.

Bed A
YEAR 1 Cabbage family and lettuce.
YEAR 2 Potatoes and root crops.
YEAR 3 Onion family and pea family.

Bed B
YEAR 1 Onion family and pea family.
YEAR 2 Cabbage family and lettuce.
YEAR 3 Potatoes and root crops.

Bed C
YEAR 1 Potatoes and root crops.
YEAR 2 Onion family and pea family.
YEAR 3 Cabbage family and lettuce.

Buying and growing vegetables

Garden centres have begun to sell a range of vegetable plants in spring. By starting off with small plants rather than seed you will save yourself the chores of sowing and pricking out, however, your choice of varieties will be restricted.

Mail-order seed catalogues offer a wider range of bolt-resistant and disease-resistant varieties than you will find in garden centres. You can also get any seed ordering and planning completed in winter. Any unsown seed from previous years can be used – apart from parsnip seed – if it has been kept cool and dry in an airtight tin.

Sow seed in modular trays so that each seedling has plenty of space to grow. This will also make transferring seedlings from trays into pots unnecessary. Young plants started off indoors will need 'hardening off' – to get used to colder conditions – before they can cope with being outside. The easiest way to do this is in a cold frame. Place plants in the cold frame with the lid just slightly open for a few hours during the day. Close the lid and cover with a double layer of garden fleece at night. Over a ten-day period, open the lid wider for longer periods during the day. If you do not have a cold frame, stand your plants outside on fine days, but bring them in at night, for two or three weeks before planting. Plants from garden centres may also need hardening off, so check when you buy them.

■ **Planting** Apply a balanced general feed, such as blood, fish and bone, or Growmore to the soil a few weeks before planting. Vegetables that are not fully hardy should be planted out after the last frost (usually between mid May and early June). Water the plants thoroughly in their pots (add a dilute liquid feed if they have been in the pots for several weeks). When planting, lay a marked stick on the soil to make spacing easier. Water again after planting and mulch.

■ **Aftercare** Once the key time-consuming tasks of digging, watering and weeding have been streamlined, aftercare of all crops takes much less time. Fast-growing crops may need a second application of balanced fertiliser during the growing season; sprinkle the fertiliser between the rows and hoe or water in.

■ **Harvesting** Harvest courgettes and mangetout peas early. Pick over runner beans regularly to keep them producing. Root crops and cabbages can be left on the plot for weeks, even months before they are picked. Onions, garlic, shallots and winter squashes must be dried off in the sun before storing.

Storage

Many vegetables can be kept for use in winter by simple storage. Damaged vegetables should be used fresh.

■ **Storing dry** After drying, store onions, shallots and garlic in a frost-free shed or garage. Store only those that are firm and keep them in net bags hung up so the air can circulate around them. Potatoes, provided they are kept in the dark, and winter squashes can also be stored like this.

■ **Freezing** Only top-quality, fresh produce is worth freezing, so aim to pick and freeze the same day. Freeze leaf beet, baby carrots, french beans, calabrese and broccoli.

■ **Storing in the ground** Beetroot, brussels sprouts, carrots, kale, leeks, parsnips and winter cabbages can be left on the plot in winter, but cover them with cloches to prevent the soil from freezing.

ALL PLANTS NEED ENOUGH WATER TO SURVIVE, WHICH MEANS THAT ARTIFICIAL WATERING IS USUALLY NECESSARY DURING DRY SPELLS. WITH SUPPLIES OFTEN RUNNING LOW IN SUMMER, IT MAKES SENSE TO USE WATER AS WISELY AS POSSIBLE IN THE GARDEN, BOTH FOR ENVIRONMENTAL REASONS AND TO SAVE MONEY ON METERED SUPPLIES.

Conserving water

Well-established plants in the ground should be able to survive all but severe drought without extra water, so concentrate watering on those plants that must not be allowed to dry out. The key to successful plant survival starts way back at the soil preparation and planting stage, with the addition of organic matter to the soil; this improves its water-holding capacity as it acts like a sponge.

You should also 'lock in' valuable moisture by mulching the ground every spring to reduce evaporation from the soil. Apply a 5-8cm layer of organic material such as chipped bark, garden compost or well-rotted manure. Work in co-operation with nature: if you garden on free-draining, fast-drying soil, opt for drought-tolerant plants that thrive in such sites.

Watering techniques

■ **In hot weather,** water in the evening or early morning, which is when less moisture is lost by evaporation, and when plants can take up water more efficiently. This also avoids the danger of water-splashed leaves becoming scorched in bright sunshine.

■ **In cooler seasons,** water early in the day so that the foliage then has a chance to dry out, as moist leaves provide an attractive environment for disease. This is particularly important for plants growing under cover.

■ **How you water** is also important. Water the soil – not the plant. During the growing season, always give plants a thorough soaking as a sprinkling of water can be more harmful than none at all, encouraging roots to quest towards the surface.

Recycling and saving water

■ **Collecting rainwater in a water butt** is one way to reduce your use of mains water – many plants prefer it. Models range from inexpensive standard plastic butts to wooden ones or slim wall-mounted models. If looks do not matter, any large watertight container will do, like plastic barrels thrown out from factories or an old water tank. Make sure it has not previously contained anything toxic that could harm your plants.

Priority plants

In dry weather, concentrate on watering those plants that need it most.

■ **New plants** Do not allow these to dry out during their first year, as they will not have established enough of a root system to take up sufficient moisture.

■ **New lawns** Whether they have been made from seed or turf, new lawns need to be kept moist for several months until established. Fine lawns also need watering regularly throughout their lives. Existing general-purpose lawns can be left to their own devices – despite turning brown, they will green up quickly once rain arrives.

■ **Annuals and newly sown seed** These must not dry out for the first few weeks after planting; after that you can get away with an occasional soaking during dry spells, with the exception of thirsty plants like sweet peas that prefer regular watering.

■ **Plants in containers** You will need to water these frequently, even daily, in summer.

■ **Vegetables** To produce good crops, all vegetables benefit from regular watering, particularly leafy vegetables such as salad crops and spinach, and those with large or succulent fruits such as tomatoes or courgettes.

■ **Soft fruit** Strawberries and raspberries need watering while the fruit is developing.

■ You can use recycled or 'grey' water from baths and sinks on the garden if it is fairly clean and free from strong detergents. Water from washing machines and dishwashers, however, is not suitable.

Watering patios

Plants in pots have a limited root area from which to take up moisture, compounded by an 'umbrella' of foliage that keeps most rainfall off the compost. The frequency of watering can be reduced by using water-retaining gels, self-watering containers and large pots. You can cut the workload dramatically by installing a watering system; the addition of a timer will make the system completely automatic.

Choosing containers

The size and type of container and the amount of plant growth it has to support, influences how quickly compost dries out. Hanging baskets dry out fastest and pots of porous material like terracotta also dry out quicker – but you can reduce water loss by lining the inside of the container (not the base) with polythene.

If you don't want to bother with a watering system, opt for large containers and put a selection of plants in each one, rather than having lots of smaller pots.

Self-watering containers incorporate a built-in reservoir, a design is particularly useful for hanging baskets.

Patio watering systems

A basic design consists of a rigid hose running to the area to be watered. Flexible microbore tubing travels from the hose to the containers, delivering water to each pot by means of an attached drip nozzle. The hose itself connects to a tap which you turn on manually, or you can fit a water timer to make the system automatic. A watering system is perfect for containers as the water is delivered slowly and gently. Although fairly costly and time-consuming to set up, such a system can last for years, save time and keep your plants in glowing good health all summer – even during holidays.

Compost and water-retaining gel

Soil-based compost is the best type to use for all permanent plants as it is best at retaining water. Improve the water-holding capacity of soil-less compost by using water-retaining gel, made up of granules that swell to many times their own size when wet. Mix just a small quantity of the dry granules into the compost before potting – or you can buy compost that already contains the gel. Make sure you water frequently, because once the gel has given up its store of moisture, the compost dries out very quickly. Do not use gel for containers that are outside in autumn, winter or early spring, as the compost would become too wet and cold.

Automatic watering systems

■ **Make your watering system fully automatic** by fitting an automatic or computer operated timer. The former is designed to water once a day and is relatively inexpensive, while a computer gives much greater flexibility of watering times but costs almost twice as much.

■ **The frequency and length** of the watering period will vary, depending on the site and weather conditions. If you are planning to go on holiday, set up the timer at least a week in advance and monitor the amount of watering required to keep the container compost evenly moist but not waterlogged. The best time to set up a watering system is during hot weather when the pipes will be soft and flexible.

■ **In winter, make sure the system is drained of water**, which could otherwise freeze and cause damage. Ideally, it should be dismantled and stored under cover, with open ends of pipes sealed with tape to prevent insects crawling in and creating blockages next year. Timers should be dried and stored with their batteries removed.

REMOVE ANNUAL WEEDS BEFORE THEY SET SEED BECAUSE SEEDS CAN STAY IN THE SOIL FOR YEARS AND MAY GERMINATE WHENEVER THE SOIL IS DUG OVER. PERENNIAL WEEDS NEED TO BE CAUGHT EARLY AND REMOVED BEFORE THEIR ROOT SYSTEMS HAVE A CHANCE TO SPREAD.

A weed is any plant growing in the wrong place. Many native wild flowers would be classed as weeds when growing among border plants or vegetables, but would be welcomed in a wild flower meadow, while cultivated narcissi and tulips would not look out of place in a garden, but would be quite unacceptable – and therefore technically weeds – in a native wild flower meadow.

Organic methods of control

The best way to control weeds is to keep on top of them. If you start with clean soil, you can hoe off or pull out all seedling weeds as they appear so they never get the chance to become established. Mulching with chipped bark, cocoa shell, stone chippings and gravel, especially if a weed barrier sheet or black polythene is laid on the soil first, will slow down weed regrowth, but seedlings eventually appear in mulches and must be removed immediately. You can singe the tops of weeds off with a gas flame gun, but this is only effective on very young ones, which are as easily pulled out or hoed off.

Established perennial weeds can be more difficult to eliminate. If you are prepared to wait, covering the soil with heavy gauge black polythene will smother the majority of weeds within twelve months, but some

Common annual weeds

CHICKWEED (1) A low-mat up to 30cm across. Hoe or hand weed to remove stems which can re-root.

CLEAVERS (2) Hoe in early spring before it seeds in summer. Stems reach several feet and are covered with sticky hairs. Adult plants are difficult to disentangle from other plants.

GROUNDSEL (3) Hoe in dry weather when small. Seeds will germinate throughout the year. Adult weed produces small, yellow, dandelion-like flowers and grows 23-40cm.

HAIRY BITTERCRESS (4) Can flower and set seed very quickly so hoe seedlings immediately – from late spring to autumn. Flower spikes reach about 20cm from small leaf rosettes.

DEAD NETTLE, RED (5) Hoe seedlings that appear in spring and autumn. Mature plants grow to 45cm and produce red or purple flowers all summer.

FAT HEN (6) Hoe seedlings that appear throughout the growing season. Hand weed older plants which have triangular leaves and reach 90cm tall. Seed is long-lived.

IVY-LEAVED SPEEDWELL (7) Hoe seedlings that appear over winter starting in October. By April sprawling stems are covered in tiny pale blue flowers. Seed dispersed by ants.

KNOTGRASS (8) Hoe or hand weed seedlings in spring and early summer. If left, plants will grow to 60cm and flower any time between July and October.

Common perennial weeds

BINDWEED (1) Hoe often or use a systemic weedkiller in spring before plants climb and wind around other plants. White or pink flowers in summer.

DANDELION (2) Hoe seedlings that appear in April/June. Large plants need to be dug out or killed with a spot weedkiller. Take action before the plant sets seed.

DOCK, BROAD LEAVED (3) Seedlings appear throughout the growing season. Hoe them or dig them out when they are bigger. Otherwise spot treat with a systemic weedkiller. Older plants can reach up to 90cm tall.

GREATER PLANTAIN (4) Hoe out seedlings when they appear in spring and autumn. Flowers in its first year. Plants can reach 30cm. Seed is long-lived.

COUCH GRASS (5) Hoe out seedlings when they appear in summer. Once plants are established use systemic weedkiller. Plants can reach 75cm tall.

JAPANESE KNOTWEED (6) A real problem weed once it is established. In the early stages it can be dug out. Use a systemic weedkiller on mature plants. Repeat as necessary.

CREEPING BUTTERCUP (7) Hoe seedlings from spring to autumn. Once established, dig out by hand, or spot treat with systemic weedkiller.

STINGING NETTLE (8) Hoe out young seedlings which appear throughout the growing season. Dig out older plants, or spot treat with systemic weedkiller. Leave some to attract wildlife. Seed is long-lived.

stubborn ones, like ground elder, Japanese knotweed and couch grass, may take much longer. Digging them out is much quicker, but some weeds, like bindweed and horsetail, are difficult to remove entirely as every little piece left behind will re-grow.

Using herbicides (weedkillers)

Weedkillers, used correctly, are a highly efficient way of removing weeds. Selective weedkillers eliminate a certain category of weeds, and are generally found in lawn treatments containing the chemicals 2,4-D and mecoprop-p. Soil applied herbicides, such as dichlobenil and sodium chlorate, kill roots and emerging growth, and are usually restricted to path weed control or around woody plants where you wish to keep the soil clean for a long period. Foliage applied weedkillers either kill weeds by contact, like

paraquat and diquat, or by translocation, when the plant absorbs the chemical through the leaf and takes it down to the roots, like glyphosate, which is perhaps the most widely used of all weedkillers at present as, applied correctly, is highly efficient and once the weeds are dead, the ground can be replanted immediately. In addition there are woody plant and stump killers, such as ammonium sulphamate, which can be used to kill and rot off the stump when a tree is felled.

Take care! Read the instructions carefully. Make sure you have the right product for your job and apply strictly according to the manufacturer's guidelines. Always apply weedkillers on a still day and keep animals and children well away for the recommended time. Keep a watering can or sprayer specifically for weed control. Store in a safe place and never decant from their original containers.

Pruning for better results

Prune little and often to keep your plants under control and in good health; if left for years, it will build up into a massive task. Not all shrubs have to be pruned each year, but they should be checked and lightly pruned if untidy.

When pruning, make as clean a cut as possible to avoid damaging the plant. Try to prune to an outward-facing bud or pair of buds. On shrubs with lots of thin stems, such as *Lonicera nitida*, *Spiraea japonica* and *Potentilla fruticosa*, it is not easy or practical to make such a precise cut, so to save time prune them with garden shears. After a few weeks of growth, they will lose their stark appearance.

Rejuvenating an old shrub

Old, overgrown shrubs can be rejuvenated by pruning them over several seasons. In the first year, in early spring, cut out a quarter to a third of the old wood as low down in the plant as possible. This will

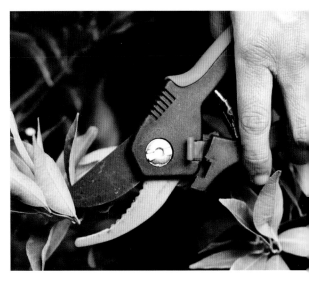

encourage strong new shoots to grow. When the new growth is at its maximum – probably in midsummer – trim it back by a third to make the plant bushier. In the second year, cut back the remaining old wood to leave only the new growth from the previous season.

Pruning tips

- Make as clean a cut as possible.
- Prune out all dead, diseased or damaged wood before starting to prune to shape.
- Cut out any frost-damaged shoots once frost-free weather has arrived.
- Remove all-green shoots on variegated shrubs to avoid them taking over the plant.
- Cut down eucalyptus to near ground level each spring, once frosts are over, to give a constant supply of fresh, young foliage.
- Don't worry about pruning to a bud if the plant has thin, wiry stems.
- Don't prune on wet, cold days, because wet foliage makes the job unpleasant.
- Choose a fine, dry day.
- Don't prune if in doubt or unless the shrub really needs it.

Pruning tools

Three types of tool will cope with all normal pruning needs for shrubs and small trees.
- **Secateurs** (either anvil or bypass types) are used for pruning most shrubs and evergreen hedging plants.
- **A pair of long-handled loppers** are needed for cutting thick shoots and branchlets on shrubs and small trees.
- **A pruning saw** is necessary for cutting off large branches.

! Keep all your pruning tools clean and sharp so that they work efficiently. To avoid the danger of spreading diseases, it is advisble to clean secateurs with a garden steriliser after use.

Pruning shrubs

Pruning to remove any dead, damaged or diseased wood – the three Ds – can generally be done at any time of year. If you buy well-shaped shrubs you shouldn't need to prune them for the first three to five years.

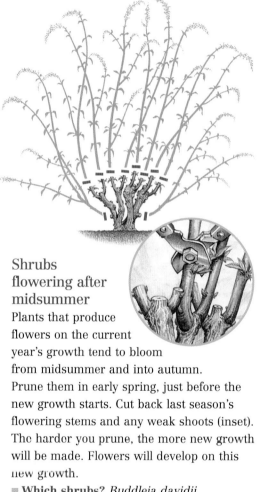

Shrubs flowering after midsummer

Plants that produce flowers on the current year's growth tend to bloom from midsummer and into autumn. Prune them in early spring, just before the new growth starts. Cut back last season's flowering stems and any weak shoots (inset). The harder you prune, the more new growth will be made. Flowers will develop on this new growth.

■ **Which shrubs?** *Buddleja davidii*, *Carypteris* x *clandonesis*, *Ceanothus* x *delileanus* 'Gloire de Versailles', *Ceratostigma willmottianum*, hebes (large-leaved types), *Hydrangea paniculata*, lavatera, *Potentilla fruticosa*, *Spiraea japonica*.

Shrubs flowering before midsummer

Plants that produce flowers on the previous year's growth bloom mainly in spring and early summer. Prune as soon as the flowers fade. Cut out a quarter to a third of older flowering shoots, cutting back to the highest new shoot or bud (inset). The plant will then make new growth in summer that will produce flowers the following spring.

■ **Which shrubs?** Deutzia, escallonia, exochorda, *Forsythia* x *intermedia*, such as *F.* x *intermedia* 'Lynwood', *Kerria japonica*, *Kolkwitzia amabilis*, philadelphus, *Prunus triloba*, *Ribes sanguineum*, *Spiraea* 'Arguta', weigela.

Young foliage or coloured stems

Some shrubs are grown for their attractive new foliage or coloured stems. Prune these in early spring to encourage lush new growth for summer and brighter stems for winter. Prune back all of the previous year's growth to near

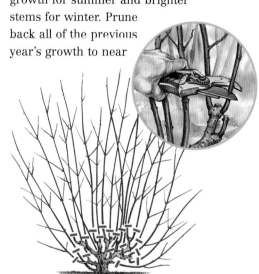

ground level or back to an established framework of branches.

■ **Which shrubs?** *Cornus alba* and *C. stolonifera, Rubus cockburnianus, Salix alba* and *S. daphnoides*. Also shrubs with attractive young foliage, such as varieties of *Sambucus nigra, Philadelphus coronarius* 'Aureus' and *Spiraea japonica* 'Goldflame'.

Evergreen foliage

Prune shrubs that are grown mainly for their evergreen foliage when they need to be kept in shape. Best times to prune are late spring and summer. Avoid pruning in frosty weather because this can cause frost damage. Cut out unwanted shoots to maintain shape and size (inset). Shorten over-long shoots and thin congested plants.

■ **Which shrubs?** *Elaeagnus pungens*, such as *E. pungens* 'Maculata' and *E.* x *ebbingei, Griselinia littoralis, Lonicera nitida, Photinia* x *fraseri*, such as *P.* x *fraseri* 'Red Robin', *Prunus laurocerasus, Prunus lusitanica, Viburnum tinus* (some flowers may be lost).

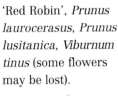

Evergreens – trimming made easy

Low-growing and ground-cover shrubs planted near to a path will need occasional trimming. An easy technique to prune them while maintaining their natural shape is to lift the growth off the path and cut out the lower shoots back to near the centre of the plant.

When the existing stems are lowered back onto the ground, they will cover the cuts made beneath.

■ Keep in shape. Cut back the remaining top shoots by shortening them slightly to keep the overall shape of the plant.

Pruning roses

Hybrid teas and floribundas need 'proper' pruning only once a year, the time depending on your garden's exposure. If you have a sheltered garden, prune just before growth starts in late February or early March. If your garden is exposed to strong winter winds, shorten long stems in early winter to prevent the roses being damaged by rocking. Then prune properly in late March.

You can use the same technique to prune both hybrid tea and floribunda roses (see over). Established shrub roses need to be pruned only once a year, and in the first year or two, a few of the longest shoots may be shortened by a third to encourage new, bushy growth. And miniature and patio roses are best pruned in late spring, once the frosty season is over, using secateurs or scissors to snip off any dead or frost-damaged shoots and if necessary thin crowded stems. Of all types of roses, though, ground-cover ones are easiest to maintain because they need pruning only if straggly.

Rose pruning made easy

As for other woody plants, cut out all dead and diseased wood, and open up the centre of the bush; but this does not have to be done every year.

■ **Trim ground-cover roses** If they become straggly or out of control, cut back ground-cover roses with a pair of shears in early spring, removing upward-growing stems and thinning overcrowded growth.

■ **Quick prune floribundas/hybrid teas** Cut across at a height of 15-20cm with a hedge trimmer in early spring. Every few years, use secateurs to clear away weak and dead shoots in the base (below).

■ **Keep shrub roses in shape (top right)** Once established, pruning need be done only every two years – in early winter or spring. Thin out a few old shoots and trim back untidy growth to maintain a good shape.

Trimming flowers and foliage

Most plants bloom for longer and produce more flowers if faded blooms are removed. The time taken deadheading can be reduced by using a pair of shears when possible. Combine this with the removal of tired-looking foliage on bushy, low-growing plants, including lady's mantle (*Alchemilla mollis*), *Astrantia major* 'Sunningdale Variegated', *Lamium maculatum* 'White Nancy' or 'Pink Pewter', catmint (*Nepeta cataria*), golden feverfew (*Tanacetum parthenium* 'Aureum') and *pulmonaria*. Clip back close to ground level then water and feed them to stimulate the production of replacement foliage and flowers.

Clipping some bedding and herbaceous plants, including *Erigeron karvinskianus*, petunias, *Senecio cineraria* and *Viola cornuta*, can stimulate another flush of flowers. In the case of plants that produce branched flower spikes, such as foxgloves, delphiniums, penstemons and snapdragons, old spikes can be cut off at the base as the flowers fade in order to encourage a second flush of flowers that appear later in summer.

Do not be too quick to cut down plants in autumn, however, unless you need to control self-seeding. The winter skeletons of many plants, such as astilbe and eryngium, can be very attractive, especially when they are covered in frost. Also, the top growth and leaf litter helps to protect the crowns of more tender plants, such as agapanthus, phygelius and hardy fuchsias. Clear away any remaining top growth in spring before new buds start to break into growth. For tender plants, such as dahlias, cut back the top growth and cover crowns with an insulating layer of compost, leaf-mould or bark chippings. In cold regions and on poorly drained soils, lift tender plants and store them in a dry, frost-free place until replanted in spring.

Easy hedge trimming

Reduce the amount of hedge trimming needed by spraying the hedge once a year, after trimming, with a growth regulator. This will prevent extension growth and make the hedge thicker so that even a vigorous hedge will need trimming just once a year, at the end of summer. The spray is suitable for privet and many other popular, fast-growing hedging plants. Buying or hiring powered equipment will make the job of trimming hedges faster and easier, although large-leaved plants are best clipped with secateurs. The model that you choose will depend on whether you have access to a power source and the size of the hedge. Provided the space isn't confined, use longer blades for quicker cutting. Gloves and goggles are recommended for safety regardless of the method used, and long trousers and tough boots or shoes for powered trimmers.

Hard pruning

If a hedge has grown out of hand, it is usually possible to cut it back hard in mid or late spring and start again. You will need to feed and mulch plants in the season before cutting back and in the season that follows. For deciduous hedges, cut back all twiggy growth on one side of the hedge to the main stems in winter or early spring. Wait a year and, if growth is good, do the same on the other side. Top-dress the surrounding soil with a general fertiliser, such as Growmore, and apply a mulch to help the plant to make a good recovery. For evergreen hedges, carry out the work in mid or late spring. Hedging plants that respond well to this treatment include deciduous beech, berberis, hawthorn and hornbeam, and evergreen holly, box-leaved honeysuckle (*Lonicera nitida*), privet, yew and cherry laurel (*Prunus laurocerasus*). Such drastic cutting is not suitable, though, for many conifers.

Coping with overgrown leylandii

It is not uncommon for a Leyland cypress hedge to reach 9m or more. This makes Leyland hedges time-consuming and awkward to trim. For a drastic remedy, you can cut them down to a metre high, and hope that they recover. They can also be rescued if they go brown at the base. Get professional help if the hedge is 3m or more above the height of your stepladder.

■ **Grown too tall** In late spring, cut down the main trunk to a height of 1m. For safety, do this in several stages if the hedge is tall. It's possible that the hedge will not recover, but then it will be at a manageable height to uproot.

■ **Brown at the base** For a quick way to cover up any dead, lower branches that have turned brown, plant periwinkle (vinca) or ivy at the base of the hedge — both these plants are able to cope with the dry, shady conditions cast by dense evergreen hedges.

110 Propagation techniques

YOU CAN MULTIPLY THE PLANTS IN YOUR GARDEN AT ALMOST NO COST BY SOWING SEED OR BY TAKING PIECES OF LEAF, STEM OR ROOT FROM YOUR EXISTING STOCK AND GROWING THEM INTO YOUNG PLANTS. OTHER TECHNIQUES INCLUDE DIVISION AND USING RUNNERS AND SUCKERS. SOME HOUSEPLANTS ARE ALSO GROWN FROM LEAF CUTTINGS.

Propagation from cuttings

Cuttings can be taken from most parts of a plant, but the techniques vary according to the time of year. Different plants respond better to different methods. Always take cuttings only from healthy, well-established plants. In general, the younger and softer the material, the faster it will root.

Root cuttings from perennials

Herbaceous perennials are often propagated by division (see page 114), but root cuttings are an excellent alternative. During late autumn or winter, pieces of root are removed and replanted. The method is suitable for shrubs and perennials that have fleshy roots, including bergenias, romneyas and oriental poppies. Do not take root cuttings from grafted plants; only the rootstock will grow.

1 During autumn or winter, lift the plant, wash off the soil and remove a root. Then replant the parent plant.

2 Cut thick or fleshy roots, as found on dicentras, oriental poppies and romneyas, into pieces 5-7.5cm long. Trim off any excess fibrous roots. Cut the upper end – nearest the plant – straight across and cut the lower end at a slant. This is in order to distinguish the top from the bottom when you put the cutting in the compost. Cut thin-rooted plants, such as phlox and verbascums, into 5cm pieces.

3 Fill a large pot with equal parts of peat and horticultural sand. For thick cuttings, make planting holes 5cm apart, and about 5-7.5cm deep. Insert each cutting, slanted end down, until the flat top is flush with the surface of the compost. Cover with 5mm of sand. Leave the pot of cuttings in a closed cold frame during winter.

With thin cuttings, lay them flat on the surface of a seed tray filled with cuttings compost and cover with a layer of compost. Leave them in a closed cold frame throughout winter.

4 Pot the rooted cuttings individually in spring, when they have developed three or four pairs of leaves and also some roots which develop after the leaves. Up to this point water sparingly, if at all. Put each one in an 8cm pot of John Innes No.1 compost or a soilless equivalent and return them to the cold frame. Stand them outdoors through summer, and plant them in their flowering positions in autumn.

Basal cuttings for perennials

Basal cuttings are taken of soft new growth from herbaceous perennials, just as it emerges from the soil. The technique is used for plants which become hollow-stemmed later in the season, such as dahlias, delphiniums and chrysanthemums.

1 In spring, when the young shoots at the base of the plant are about 10cm long, cut them off at crown level or just below.

2 Plant individually in 8cm pots, filled with cuttings compost or equal parts of sand and peat and put them in a cold frame.

3 Keep the cuttings well watered by spraying from overhead, and keep the frame closed. About six weeks later, pot the cuttings singly in 8cm pots of John Innes No.1 compost or soilless potting compost. Keep them in the cold frame until frosts have finished. Plant them in their flowering positions in autumn.

Softwood cuttings for perennials

Softwood cuttings are immature, soft shoot tips in the first flush of growth, taken in April or May. The method is commonly used for hardy herbaceous perennials and greenhouse plants, as well as fuchsias and hydrangeas. Cuttings will root best in a warm propagating case with heating cables in the bottom.

Softwood cuttings wilt quickly; get all the materials ready before taking the cuttings so that they can be inserted into the compost immediately. Take the cuttings in the morning and put them straight into a polythene bag.

1 Softwood cuttings should be young and non-flowering, just firm but not hard, and about 7.5cm long. Remove a shoot that has four or five pairs of leaves.

2 Using a craft knife or garden knife, slice the bottom off the shoot, just below the lowest pair of leaves. Without damaging the stem, pull off the bottom two pairs of leaves. Then dip the base of the cutting in hormone rooting powder – preferably one that contains a fungicide.

3 Fill a 13cm pot with cuttings compost to just below the rim. Alternatively, use a mixture of equal parts (by volume) of peat

and horticultural sand. The pot will take up to ten cuttings around the edge, according to their size. Using a pointed stick or a pencil, make holes in the compost about a third the length of the cuttings.

4 Insert each cutting in a hole and press it in place. Water them in, using a fungicidal solution to prevent rot. Keep the cuttings in a propagator (preferably with bottom heat), covered and shaded.

5 When the cuttings have rooted – after about a month – pot them individually in 8cm pots of potting compost. Keep them watered and shaded until they have become established. Plant them in their flowering positions the following spring.

Greenwood cuttings for shrubs and sub-shrubs

Greenwood cuttings are taken in early summer when the bottom end of the cutting is just beginning to ripen. Greenwood cuttings are slightly slower to root than softwood cuttings, but are less prone to wilt. Greenwood cuttings are taken from the soft tip of a stem when spring growth has started to slow – about the beginning of June. The lower stem is firm but not hard. The technique is used for ericas, lantanas, pelargoniums and chrysanthemums.

1 Take the cuttings early in the morning and put them in a plastic bag – if they start to dry out they may not root.

2 Use a garden knife to trim the cuttings to about 7.5-10cm long. Cut the leaves from the lower half of the cutting. Dip the cut end in a hormone rooting powder of softwood strength, preferably containing a fungicide.

3 Almost fill a 13cm pot with cuttings compost. Make small holes in the compost around the edge of the pot, and insert the cuttings up to the leaves. Then firm them in.

4 Put the pot in a covered propagating case, preferably with bottom heat, or beneath a polythene tent to prevent dehydration. Ensure the cuttings have plenty of light, but shade them from direct sunlight.

5 Repot the young plants individually in 8cm pots of potting compost. Plant them in their flowering positions the following spring.

6 After five to eight weeks the cuttings should have rooted and they can be gradually hardened off by increasing the level of ventilation.

Semi-ripe cuttings for shrubs

Many shrubs root well from semi-ripe material taken from mid July to the end of August – earlier in very hot summers. Some examples are actinidia, choisya, lavandula, philadelphus and weigela. Semi-ripe cuttings are taken in July or August when most of the stem is fresh and green but the bottom end is turning ripe and brown. They need to be rooted in warm conditions in a cold frame or propagating case.

1 The cuttings are taken from the current year's growth – the tips of the shoots are soft but the lower stem is firm. Remove 15-20cm long, non-flowering sideshoots with leaves growing on them. Take off the leaves from the lower part of the shoot and sever it just below a leaf joint. Cut off the soft tip above a leaf to leave a cutting 5-10cm long.

2 Use an 8cm pot for up to five cuttings, a 13cm pot for from five to ten. Almost fill with cuttings compost. Dip the base of the cutting in a hormone rooting agent.

Make holes in the compost around the edge of the pot, but make sure the leaves will not touch. Insert each cutting to a third

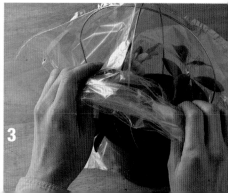

Taking heeled cuttings

Some semi-ripe cuttings will root more strongly if they are removed from the shrub with a heel-like sliver of the previous year's wood attached. This heel helps roots to form because it surrounds the base of the new growth, an area rich in the plant's growth hormones. Cut off a main shoot that has several sideshoots – preferably without flowers. Pull off a sideshoot, or make a slanting cut into the main stem below the junction with the sideshoot; then cut in the opposite direction to remove the shoot.

Ripewood cuttings for evergreens

Evergreen shrubs are often propagated from ripewood cuttings which are taken in late summer or early autumn. The cuttings are planted in a cold frame or propagator and left over winter. Aucuba, escallonia and hebe can be reproduced in this way.

1 Take heel cuttings (see box, left) in late summer from a stem of the current season's growth. Trim the leaves off the bottom third and pinch out the tip.

With plants that are difficult to root – such as daphne and eleagnus – cut a 2.5cm long shallow vertical groove in the stem. Dip the cut end in a rooting hormone powder of ripewood strength and cover the groove with the powder.

2 Dig the soil in a cold frame thoroughly and add a mixture of peat and sand. Plant each cutting up to its leaves. Be sure that the leaves of adjacent cuttings are not touching or they may rot. Close the lid securely and keep the plants shaded. Remove the shading as the days grow shorter. In cold weather, insulate the frame with carpet, blanket or newspapers.

3 Grow the shrubs on for another year in individual pots. Then plant them out in spring.

of its length and firm the compost. Water well, preferably using a fungicidal solution.

3 To prevent the cuttings drying out, a humid atmosphere is essential. Fit a plastic bag over the pot, supported by two hoops of galvanised wire. Water the cuttings and put them in a draught-free, warm and shaded place such as a cold frame or propagator. Rooting is faster with bottom heat.

4 Once the cuttings have rooted, harden them off by making a few holes in the plastic bag to let air in. Slit the bag a week later. Another week after that you can remove the cover completely.

5 Remove the rooted cuttings and carefully separate them with a plant label or pencil. Then pot each young plant in an 8cm pot of potting compost. Water them in, and do not allow the compost to dry out.

Keep the pots under cover and harden off in spring when the young plants can be planted out or transferred to larger pots.

Helping evergreens to stay moist

Cuttings of evergreen shrubs and trees may dry out as they lose moisture through their leaves. And this will cause them to fail. To prevent evaporation, you can put the cuttings in a cold frame and spray them with an antidesiccant spray, such as a Christmas-tree spray. But best of all, if you have a greenhouse, install a mist propagating unit which maintains the moisture level automatically.

Hardwood cuttings for trees and shrubs

The easiest way of growing new deciduous shrubs or trees is to take hardwood cuttings in late autumn or early winter – ideally in October or early November. After the cuttings have been planted, little attention is needed for the next 12 months when the new young plants are moved to their permanent positions. Before taking the cuttings, choose a patch of soil sheltered from north and east winds, and dig it thoroughly – if the soil is clay dig in horticultural sand or grit and organic matter to help with drainage.

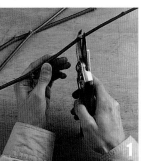

1 Choose a shoot that has just completed its first season's growth. Use a sharp knife or secateurs to cut it from the plant close to the main stem. Trim the cutting just below a bud at the base and just above a bud at the top so that it is about 25cm long.

2 To encourage the cutting to root, remove a thin sliver of bark near the base on one or both sides, using a sharp knife. Lightly dip the base and the wounded strips into hormone rooting compound.

3 Make a narrow V-shaped trench in the prepared soil by pushing in a spade to its full depth and pulling it forwards. Spread horticultural sand 2.5cm deep in the bottom of the trench and stand the cuttings on it, 10cm apart, so that half or two-thirds of each cutting is below ground. Fill the trench with soil and tread it firm.

4 In early spring tread the soil firm if it has been lifted by frost. Keep the area free of weeds, and water during dry spells throughout spring and summer. Some plants, including populus, salix, cornus and ribes, will be ready to be moved to their permanent sites, or potted up, the following autumn. But if little growth has been made, leave the cuttings for another year.

Increasing perennials by division

The easiest way of propagating herbaceous perennials is by division, which involves lifting a plant from the soil and separating it into two or more pieces. Each piece when replanted will grow as an identical plant to the parent. Division is not only used to increase the number of plants, but also to perpetuate existing stocks which are beginning to deteriorate or become overcrowded.

Division is done between October and April, but not when the soil is frozen or sticky. Perennials that flower early in the year are best divided in autumn.

Fibrous-rooted plants

1 Once the plant has been lifted, force the prongs of two garden forks into the clump, back to back. Separate the clump by first pushing the handles of the forks together.

2 Then pull them wide apart. Repeat until you have two halves, then separate the

halves. Alternatively, cut the clump into pieces
with an old knife or a sharpened spade.

3 Cut away and discard the central woody
part of each piece. Then divide the
remainder into pieces, each containing about
six buds or shoots. Discard unhealthy growth
and plant the divisions in their flowering
positions. Water well in dry weather.

Rhizomatous-rooted plants

Plants that grow from rhizomes, such as
bergenias, monardas, physalis and
polygonatum, are easily lifted – ideally in
early spring when new growth buds sprout.

1 Lift the rootstock with a garden fork and
prise off the soil to reveal the main rhizome
and the younger stems. If necessary, wash
the clump. Choose side growths about 7.5cm
long which have healthy roots and two or
three vigorous growth buds. Cut them off
with a knife.

> ### Dividing bearded irises
> Lift the plants and cut off the younger rhizomes
> from around the edge of the clump. Each
> portion of rhizome should have one or two
> strong, healthy leaves. Peel off withered
> leaves and trim the remainder to
> a fan shape to reduce
> wind rock. Then plant in
> the flowering position.

2 Discard the old rhizome and trim the cut
pieces to just below a cluster of fine healthy
roots, removing any dead material. Plant the
cut pieces, with the root cluster downwards,
at about the same depth as the original
plant. Fill in the soil and press it firmly
into place around the new plant.

Fleshy and tuberous roots

Some herbaceous perennials grow from
tubers – thickened, fleshy rootstocks or
crowns. The small
tubers of liatris and
spring-flowering
anemones are easily
pulled apart by hand.
But the large, fleshy
roots of hemerocallis
and peonies have to
be cut into pieces
with a knife.

1 Lift a clump of
plants and carefully
clean off the soil.
Wash if necessary.
This will reveal
growth buds (above, right).

2 Divide the rootstock into several pieces,
cutting through the crown from the top
downwards. Then plant at once in their
flowering positions. A piece with only one
bud takes longer to establish itself than a
section of three or four tubers and buds.
Peonies, which dislike disturbance, may take
a season or longer to recover.

Increasing shrubs and climbers by layering

Layering is a simple way of inducing the stem of a healthy plant to take root while still attached to the plant. Some trees and shrubs, such as willows and hazels, do this naturally when their stems touch the ground. Layering is a method that can succeed where cuttings fail.

Carnations and pinks are examples of herbaceous plants that respond to layering. Suitable shrubs include magnolia, viburnum, cassiope, corylopsis, heathers and many climbers, including wisteria and clematis. Deciduous plants are best layered in autumn or winter; evergreens in autumn or spring.

Ordinary layering

1 Fork over the soil near the plant – beneath the branch to be layered – and enrich it with well-rotted compost or manure. Lighten heavy soil with horticultural sand.
2 Select a vigorous, young and flexible shoot, like the one on this willow (left) and bend it down to soil level, about 25cm from its tip. Strip the leaves where the shoot touches the soil and snick the underside with a knife, cutting towards the growing tip.

3 Dig a hole 7.5-10cm beneath the wound and partly fill it with seed compost or a mixture of peat and horticultural sand. Bend a piece of galvanised wire into a hairpin and

Increasing heathers by 'dropping'

Heaths and heathers can be propagated by a form of layering called 'dropping'.
1 In late autumn or spring, dig a bowl-shaped hole deep enough to take the plant with only the tops of the branches above ground.
2 Lift the plant and put in the hole, spreading the stems in a circle so only 2.5cm is exposed.
3 Fill in the centre with a mixture of soil, sand and organic matter, working it well around each stem. Keep the soil moist and free of weeds until the following autumn. Then lift the plant, cut off those stems that have developed shoots and plant them out. Discard the parent plant.

peg the wounded stem into the hole. Cover it with compost and water thoroughly. Ensure that the compost never dries out.
4 A year later, check that the shoot has taken root by carefully scraping away the soil. If it has, sever the new plant from the parent with its rootball, and replant in its flowering position. If the roots are not yet established, replace the soil and leave for a few more months.

Serpentine layering

Climbers with long flexible stems, such as honeysuckle and jasmine, may produce three or four new plants from a single stem.
1 In autumn, choose a trailing shoot grown during the current year. Bend it down to the ground and make a small hole. Then wound the shoot by cutting a shallow tongue in the underside (cutting towards the growing tip) or twisting sharply. Pin it into the hole with bent wire and cover it with seed compost.
2 Leave the next two pairs of leaves above ground and repeat the process along the length of the shoot.
3 Firm the compost and water well. Keep the soil moist until the following autumn, when the young plants that have developed can be severed from the stem and transplanted.

Tip layering

Blackberries will produce roots from the tip of a cane if it touches the ground.

1 In summer, bend a new shoot down to the ground and tie it to a bamboo cane. Then bury the tip 12cm deep. Alternatively, tie the shoot down and plant the tip in a pot of seed compost that has been buried in the ground. Water the soil and keep it moist. A new plant should develop within a few weeks.

2 To check that roots are growing on the young plant, scrape away some of the compost. In autumn, sever it from the parent and move to a new growing position.

Air layering

Branches too stiff to bend for normal layering can be 'layered in the air'; it is used for rhododendrons and magnolias.

1 From the current year's growth, select a branch and strip off the leaves from the middle. Using a sharp knife, make a shallow cut into the stem, slicing upwards, and dust the wound with hormone rooting powder.

2 Wrap a piece of polythene around the stem below the cut to make a tube, and secure. Pack tightly with an equal mixture of moist peat, sand and sphagnum moss, and secure the top of the tube.

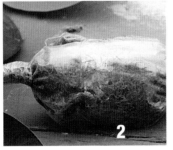

3 Between three and six months later, when the stem has rooted, cut off the stem below the roots at a leaf joint. Remove polythene.

4 Cut off the stump and put the new plant in a 13cm pot of potting compost. Keep a hardy shrub moist in a closed cold frame for two weeks and then start to harden off. Plant out in spring.

Propagation from runners and suckers

This is the easiest way of all to increase your stock. Many herbaceous plants produce a running stem on the surface with a young plant at the end (sometimes this produces another runner, with another baby) which can be pegged down into a small pot of compost to make roots, or detached at once and potted up. New roots soon form, and when they have almost filled the pot, the plant can be planted out in the garden, or in a larger container. The best example of this is the strawberry (*fragaria*).

Many shrubs produce suckers and if you dig one up, you will find a new plant with roots, still attached to the parent. In the autumn this can be removed and potted up to grow on, or removed for immediate planting. Good examples are raspberry, lilac (*syringa*), *Rosa rugosa*, *Mahonia aquifolium* (Oregon grape) snowberry (*symphoricarpos*) and poplar (*populus*). To get a good plant from a sucker, cut back top growth fairly hard after replanting. A few sub-shrubby, herbaceous perennials, such as romneya, the Californian tree poppy also produce good suckers for propagation.

As the environment is controlled by the gardener, growing under glass is more time-consuming and labour-intensive than most forms of outdoor gardening. Plants must be fed and watered, protected from the hot sun and given warmth, ventilation and humidity. The structure will need regular cleaning, particularly the glass, and the frame may require repairing or painting.

All glass structures help the gardener but a heated greenhouse offers the greatest versatility. Throughout the year a minimum temperature is maintained, enabling a wide range of plants to be grown. A cool greenhouse has a minimum temperature of 4°C and a warm greenhouse has a temperature of at least 10°C.

Glass for all purposes

The traditional greenhouse is free-standing and square or rectangular but other types may be more suitable, depending on the purpose of the greenhouse. Rounded or sloping-sided structures, such as a Dutch light greenhouse, capture more light and warmth; and circular or dome-shaped structures make good features and display ornamental plants well. A lean to, which is constructed against a wall, takes up less space and can be cheaper to heat. Alpine houses have plenty of vents and provide the cool and airy conditions in which alpine plants thrive.

■ **Glass-to-ground models** are the most versatile types; plants can be grown on and under fitted staging and indoor borders can be used for tall-growing plants like tomatoes. A greenhouse which has a solid wall to the height of the staging is more substantial and loses heat less rapidly, so may be a better choice if the structure is to be heated.

■ **A conservatory** is integral to the house, providing an extra room. Its main use is to display ornamental plants. A cold frame or walk-in polytunnel is an economical alternative to a cold greenhouse. They are used for the same purposes though cold frames do not have room for tall plants.

■ **Cloches**, which are made from glass, rigid plastic or polythene sheeting, are used outdoors to warm up the soil before planting and protect plants in cold months. They are light and easily moved.

■ **A free-standing greenhouse** or a cold frame is best sited in an open but sheltered situation. The ridge of a greenhouse should run from east to west so maximum benefit is derived from the sun in winter and spring. A lean-to should be located on a south or west-facing wall for extra warmth.

Raising plants

Raising plants from seed or cuttings under glass is cheaper than buying from garden centres or nurseries; it also allows the gardener to cultivate less common varieties.

■ **Alpines, shrubs and hardy bulbs**, perennials and vegetables can all be propagated in an unheated greenhouse or a cold frame. Hardy annuals, such as *Lathyrus odoratus* (sweet pea), can be raised in a cold greenhouse for earlier flowering than those sown outdoors.

■ **A heated greenhouse** allows more plants to be propagated, including tender crops, such as aubergines, cucumbers and tomatoes, and greenhouse pot plants, including Calceolaria and coleus.

■ **Most half-hardy annuals** and half-hardy perennials for summer bedding can also only be raised in a warm greenhouse. However, a temporary heater can be used

CREATING AN EFFICIENT GREENHOUSE

1 Shading wash Varishade shading wash is opaque when the sun shines, but turns clear when it rains to allow maximum light to get to the plants.

2 Shading External roller blinds are an efficient way of keeping a greenhouse cool, but they need to be securely fitted.

3 Automatic vents As the temperature rises, the resin-filled piston expands, forcing open the roof vents and letting out hot air.

7 Use sheets of bubble wrap to insulate the sides and roof during cold spells.

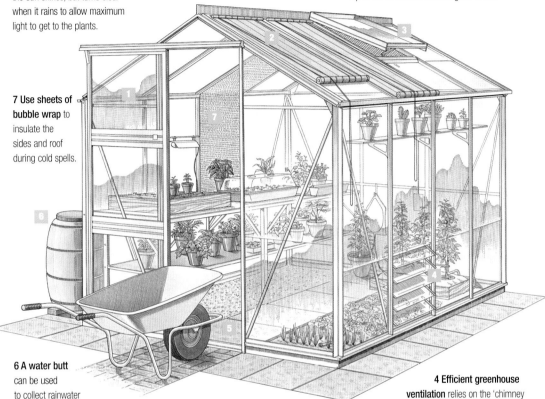

6 A water butt can be used to collect rainwater for lime-hating plants. Raise on blocks to make filling a watering can easier. Cover to prevent algae.

5 A well-designed greenhouse has an all-weather path and a door with a low threshold that is wide enough for a barrow.

4 Efficient greenhouse ventilation relies on the 'chimney effect' by which hot air rises and escapes through ridge vents and is replaced by cooler air drawn in through side vents.

in spring to increase the temperature of a cold or cool greenhouse and provide the right conditions. A few bedding plants, including Alyssum, Antirrhinum (snapdragon) and Tagetes species, can be raised in an unheated or cool greenhouse if sown in mid or late spring but will flower a few weeks later than plants raised in a warm greenhouse.

■ **A heated propagating unit** with soil-warming cables will provide the optimum germination or rooting temperatures for many plants, including summer bedding. Keep the unit and trays or pots of seeds and cuttings on the staging, which is easily accessible. The young seedlings will need plenty of light to develop; shelves in the roof space are ideal places to keep them as they receive maximum light there – although shade from the sun is vital. Harden off young plants in a cold frame, cloche or polythene tunnel before planting out.

Growing crops under glass

Tender vegetables that have a short season outdoors, such as tomatoes, peppers, cucumbers and aubergines, ripen faster and produce crops for a longer period and often of better quality under glass. Many hardy vegetables, including french beans and lettuces, also grow well and produce early or late crops in a greenhouse.

■ **Use a cold frame for cultivating low-growing vegetables**, such as lettuces and chilli peppers. In a greenhouse that has glass to the ground, use soil borders, containers or growing bags for vegetables. Make best use of space by interspersing tall plants, such as tomatoes, with smaller ones, like lettuces.

■ **Some fruits, such as figs, grapes, peaches and nectarines**, thrive under glass. They do not need high light intensity at ground level so can be cultivated in greenhouses that have solid sides up to the staging. Shade is essential for these plants so apply shading paint in spring. Grow them in containers and train a peach or nectarine tree or a grapevine onto the back wall of a lean-to.

■ **Strawberry plants** also do well under glass and give early fruits when forced in a cool or warm greenhouse.

Watering and feeding

Plants in a greenhouse need frequent watering and feeding. An automatic watering system can be useful, particularly if you spend a lot of time away. In a capillary watering system, pots stand on water-retentive fibre matting and take up moisture continuously. With trickle irrigation, each pot is supplied with a thin tube which delivers water from a main supply pipe.

■ **Watering by hand** is time consuming but enables you to water each plant according to its needs. In general, water greenhouse plants when the surface of the compost is becoming dry.

■ **All plants need less water** during their dormant periods, usually in autumn and winter. Use rainwater, collected in a butt, for any lime-hating greenhouse plants, such as camellias.

■ **Feed plants only during the growing season**. Most plants benefit from a feed every seven to fourteen days but newly potted plants should not be fed for several weeks as the compost will contain sufficient nutrients.

■ **Do not apply fertiliser** when the compost is dry, when plants are wilting due to lack of water, or in very cold weather. Some fertilisers, such as a tomato feed, are specially formulated to encourage fruit or flower production. However, a general-purpose liquid fertiliser is suitable for most plants in a greenhouse. Alternatively, insert fertiliser pellets into the compost. These release a steady supply of nutrients throughout the growing season.

Temperature and humidity

You can install permanent heating but a cheaper option is to use a small gas, electric or paraffin heater. Also available are thermostatically controlled fan heaters, which come on automatically when needed.

■ **Most greenhouses** have roof and side ventilators. When they are open, cool air is sucked in through the side vents and warm air escapes through the roof vents. Vents can be fitted with automatic openers, and electric extractor fans can also be used to improve ventilation.

■ **Ventilating the greenhouse** when the sun shines will prevent the temperature reaching a damagingly high level and keep the air fresh. It will also reduce humidity, which is vital on cold sunny days when the air should be kept dry to help to prevent disease.

■ **In spring and summer**, shading protects plants from scorching and helps to prevent excessively high temperatures. Ideally, a greenhouse or conservatory should be fitted with internal or external blinds, which allow you to shade as necessary. An alternative is to paint a liquid shading material onto the outside of the greenhouse glass in spring. Use white rather than green paint, to create more natural conditions inside. Unless it wears off naturally, remove the shading paint in autumn when plants need the maximum amount of light.

GROWING PLANTS IN YOUR GREENHOUSE

1 Sand tray Fill a sturdy box with sharp sand (not builders' sand) for rooting cuttings and watering small pots. Keep sand moist.

2 When space is short (probably in late April and early May) use temporary shelving to increase available growing space.

3 Pot tomatoes Fill big pots with growing bag compost. The greater rooting depth means plants will grow better and are easier to water.

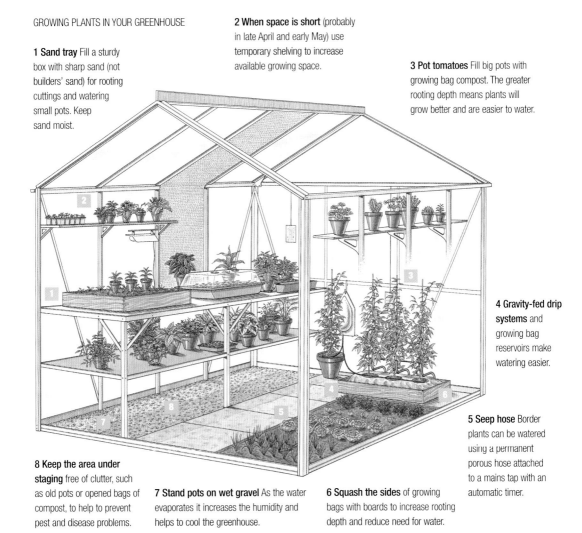

4 Gravity-fed drip systems and growing bag reservoirs make watering easier.

5 Seep hose Border plants can be watered using a permanent porous hose attached to a mains tap with an automatic timer.

6 Squash the sides of growing bags with boards to increase rooting depth and reduce need for water.

7 Stand pots on wet gravel As the water evaporates it increases the humidity and helps to cool the greenhouse.

8 Keep the area under staging free of clutter, such as old pots or opened bags of compost, to help to prevent pest and disease problems.

■ **When the temperature rises** above 15°C, damp down the floor and staging, using a watering can with a rose, or a hosepipe or sprayer. As the water evaporates, it lowers the temperature and creates humidity, which helps plants to retain water. In very warm conditions, mist plants with water. Damp down early in the morning, and several times during the day in very hot weather, if possible. Give plants time to dry off before nightfall if wetted.

■ **Start heating the greenhouse** when the weather turns cold in autumn and line the glass with clear bubble polythene to reduce heat loss. Fittings are available to hold the polythene in place, 12-25mm from the glass. Insulate ventilators with pieces of polythene cut to size so that they can still be opened. Remove insulating material in spring.

Pests and diseases

Prevent pests and diseases by maintaining hygiene. Use fresh compost and clean containers. Clean the greenhouse thoroughly once a year and keep it well-ventilated. When pests or diseases occur, act quickly as they can spread rapidly. Biological control – the use of predatory or parasitic insects or mites to control pests – is particularly effective under glass.

Glossary

WE HAVE TRIED TO AVOID TECHNICAL TERMS WHEREVER POSSIBLE THROUGHOUT THIS BOOK, BUT THEY ARE SOMETIMES UNAVOIDABLE. THE DEFINITIONS BELOW CLARIFY TERMS THAT WE HAVE USED, AND GIVE EXPLANATIONS OF OTHERS THAT YOU MAY COME ACROSS.

a

Alpine Strictly speaking, any plant that is native to mountainous regions, growing between the tree line and permanent snow line. 'Alpine' is also loosely applied to any small plant suitable for growing in a rock garden.

Annual A plant that completes its life cycle in a single growing season – from seed to flowering, to setting seed and dying.

b

Basal leaves Leaves arising directly from the crown of a plant or on a very short stem.

Biennial A plant which takes two seasons to complete its life cycle – for example, the foxglove. In year one it forms leaves; in year two it forms flowers and seeds, then dies.

Bract A modified leaf which is sometimes brightly coloured and conspicuous to attract pollinating insects, such as the scarlet bracts of poinsettia (*Euphorbia pulcherrima*).

Bulb frame A cold frame in which bulbs in pots can be plunged in sand, soil or gravel for winter to protect them from frost. A bulb frame can be used instead of an alpine house.

c

Chitting Sprouting tubers, particularly potatoes and dahlias, before planting. Also applied to seeds germinated before sowing.

Chlorosis The loss or insufficiency of chlorophyll – the green pigment in the cells of leaves and young stems. The lack of chlorophyll causes the leaves to appear bleached or yellowish. Usually due to mineral deficiency, but viruses may be a cause.

Cloche Sheets of clear glass, rigid plastic or plastic film that are used for raising early crops in open ground, and for protecting plants from bad weather – alpines, for example.

Clone A group of identical plants raised from a single parent plant by cuttings or division rather than by seed.

Compost A mixture of loam, sand, peat, leaf-mould or other materials used for growing plants in containers. Also refers to organic material obtained by stacking plant remains such as vegetable trimmings, straw and grass mowings until they decompose.

Conifer Tree or shrub, usually evergreen and having linear or needle-like leaves, and which usually bears its seeds in cones.

Coppicing The cutting back of trees and shrubs close to the ground, often annually, to produce vigorous young shoots. In gardens it is usually done for decorative purposes – to encourage brightly coloured stems or the formation of large leaves.

Corm The underground storage organ of some plants, including crocuses and gladioli. Similar to a bulb, it consists of a swollen stem with a bud at the top which produces shoots and a new corm.

Crown The part of an herbaceous perennial at soil level from which roots and shoots grow.

Cultivar Cultivated variety: a variant of a plant produced in cultivation as opposed to one that occurs in the wild.

Cuttings see page 110.

d

Damping down Watering the floor and benches of a greenhouse to create a humid atmosphere.

Deadheading Nipping off dead or faded flowerheads from a plant to prevent seeding and to encourage new flowers. Roses and many bedding plants need regular deadheading.

Dot plant An isolated or specimen plant – usually tall – in a formal flowerbed, selected to emphasise contrast in height, colour and texture.

Drill A straight narrow, furrow in which seeds are sown outdoors.

e

Ericaceous A term used for plants that grow best in acid soil, such as ericas (heather). Also used to refer to lime-free compost used for growing ericaceous plants.

Etiolated Growth which has become long, thin and pallid because of lack of light or as a result of blanching – as in forcing rhubarb.

Eye Immature growth bud, such as the eyes of potato or dahlia tubers. The term is also used to describe the centre of a flower if it is different in colour from the petals.

f

F1 hybrid Seeds obtained by crossing two pure bred closely related varieties which have been inbred for several generations. The plants tend to have an increased level of vigour and uniformity.

Feathered Lateral shoots on the main stem of a young tree. They are left on the tree until the trunk is fully established – about a year or two – when they must be removed.

Fertilisers see pages 40-45.

Floret Small individual flower that is part of a large head or cluster.

Fruiting body The reproductive organ of a fungus, such as a mushroom. Also the pinhead-like growth on bread mould.

Fumigate A system of destroying pests and diseases in a greenhouse or cold frame with poisonous fumes. Canisters or pellets are ignited to produce a dense smoke.

g

Germination The initial stage of a plant's development from a seed. Germination periods vary: given the right conditions of temperature, moisture, light and oxygen, it may occur within days or take many weeks or months.

Glabrous Smooth or bare – used to describe a part of a plant that is hairless.

Grafting Propagating plants by joining a stem or bud of one plant to the root of another so they unite to form a new individual. It is widely used in cultivating fruit trees and roses.

h

Habit The characteristic shape and growth form of a plant.

Half-hardy Frost-tender species of plants that can only be grown in the open reliably during summer – for example, canna and French and African marigolds. See also Tender.

Half-standard A tree or shrub, usually with a single stem growing 75cm–1.2 m high before the head branches.

Hardening off The gradual acclimatisation of tender and half-hardy plants, grown under protection, to outside conditions. Plants are usually placed in a cold frame in late spring, with air gradually admitted until the lights of the frame are left off entirely.

Hardy Plants which survive frosts in the open, year by year, anywhere in Great Britain.

Herbaceous Any plant that does not form a persistent woody stem. It commonly refers to perennials which die down in autumn and reappear the following spring.

Humus The dark brown residue from the final breakdown of dead vegetable matter. Often used to describe partly decayed matter that is brown and crumbly, such as well-made compost or leaf-mould.

Hybrid The result of crossing two distinct varieties or, occasionally, genera. Hybrids may either show a blending of characteristics from each parent or favour one more than the other.

Incised The margins of a leaf, stipule or bract that is deeply and sharply toothed or lobed.

Inflorescence The arrangement of flowers on a stem, often referred to as a flowerhead.

Inorganic A chemical compound or fertiliser that does not contain carbon. The term is applied to synthetically produced fertilisers, although some naturally occurring plant nutrients have inorganic origins, as, for example, the mineral fertiliser rock phosphate.

Juvenile Plants which have a distinct early phase, when either the habit, leaf shape or some other characteristic differs from those of the adult. Eucalyptus trees commonly bear juvenile and adult leaves.

Lateral A stem or shoot that branches off from a bud in the leaf axil of a larger stem.

Leader The main stem (or stems) of a tree or shrub that extends the existing branch system.

Leaf-mould Partially decayed dead leaves which have broken down to a brown, flaky condition resembling peat. Oak and beech leaves are the most suitable materials.

Lime Calcium, a chemical used in horticulture, particularly to neutralise acid soils.

Loam A reasonably fertile soil that is neither wet and sticky, nor dry and sandy. It is moisture-retentive and contains a blend of clay, silt, sand and humus, and is rich in minerals.

Maiden A nursery term for a young grafted tree in the process of being trained. Applied particularly to one-year-old fruit trees.

Mulch A layer of organic matter, such as decayed manure, leaf-mould, garden compost, straw or composted bark, which is spread on the soil around plants. A mulch conserves moisture in the soil, adds nutrients and suppresses weeds. The term is also used for inorganic material including gravel and black polythene sheeting.

Naturalising Growing plants, particularly bulbs, in simulated natural environments, such as grass or woodland conditions.

Node A stem joint, which is sometimes slightly swollen, from where young leaves and sideshoots arise.

Offset A young plant that arises naturally on the parent, as with many sorts of bulbs, or on short lateral stems, as with sempervivum.

Opposite The arrangement of leaves in alternate opposite pairs, as on ligustrum and syringa.

Organic Any chemical compound containing carbon. The term is applied to substances de-rived from the decay of living organisms, such as garden compost. It is also applied to a style of gardening that rejects the use of synthetic chemicals and products.

Perlite Lightweight expanded volcanic rock in granular form, used in place of sand or grit to open up or lighten composts used for potting or cuttings.

pH see page 29.

Pinching out see Stopping.

Plunge To set a pot or any other plant container up to the rim in the soil, or in a special bed of ashes, peat, grit or sand.

Pollard A tree cut back to the main trunk and maintained in a bushy state by regular pruning at intervals.

Pollen Male cells of a plant contained in the anthers or pollen sacs.

Pollination The transference of pollen grains onto the stigma of a flower. This may occur naturally by gravity, wind or insects, or can be done artificially by hand.

Pricking out The first planting out of seedlings or small-rooted cuttings. The resulting plantlets are later moved into larger pots, pans or trays, or set out into a nursery bed or into their growing position.

Propagation see pages 110-117.

Provenance The place where seed originated in the wild. Knowing the provenance will have a bearing on the conditions under which the progeny will thrive in cultivation.

Radical Usually used to describe the basal leaves of biennials or perennials. Leaves arise at the base of the plant or near to soil level.

Resting period The period when a plant is either dormant or making little or no extension growth.

Rhizome A horizontal, creeping underground stem, which acts as a storage organ.

Rootstock A propagation term for a plant upon which another is grafted. The term also applies to the crown and root system of herbaceous perennials and suckering shrubs.

Rosette Ring of leaves that all arise at more or less the same point on the stem, often basal.

Runner Prostrate stems, such as those produced by strawberry plants, which root at the nodes to form new plantlets.

s **Selection** A particular variation of an existing variety or species that is selected for its desirable characteristics. It is always raised from seed. Also incorrectly referred to as a 'strain'.

Self-coloured A flower having a single uniform colour.

Self-fertile A plant, particularly a fruit tree, that does not need pollen from another plant to set seed and produce fruit.

Sessile Stalkless – a leaf or flower arising straight from the stem.

Shrub A branched perennial plant with persistent woody stems.

Specimen plant Any plant, usually a tree or shrub, grown where it can be viewed from all angles, as when planted in a lawn.

Spit The depth to which soil is dug with a spade or a fork – about 25-30cm.

Spore A minute dust-like body composed of a single cell, by which lower plants – such as ferns, fungi and mosses – reproduce. A spore gives rise to an intermediate generation upon which the sex organs appear and which eventually produce plantlets.

Spur 1: A short lateral branchlet of a tree – particularly on apple and pear trees – which bears flower buds.

Spur 2: A tubular outgrowth of a sepal or petal that produces nectar.

Sterile Plants that rarely or never set seed. Many double-flowered varieties are sterile, as the reproductive organs have become petals.

Stolon A stem which, on contact with moist soil, roots at the tip and forms a new plant – for example, the cane of a blackberry. The term is sometimes incorrectly used to mean Runner.

Stool Often describing a tree or shrub which is maintained as a clump of young stems by annual pruning close to ground level.

Stooling is carried out to provide young growth for propagation purposes, or to maintain a foliage effect, such as the juvenile state of some eucalyptus. Also called 'coppicing'. The term also applies to crowns and rootstock of some herbaceous plants – dendranthema (chrysanthemum), for example.

Stopping Removing or pinching out the growing point of a stem, either to promote a branching habit or to induce flower buds.

Stratification A method of breaking the dormancy of seeds born in fleshy fruits of many hardy plants. The seeds are exposed to a period of low temperature prior to sowing.

Sub-alpine A plant native to mountain regions just below the alpine zone.

Sub-shrub A low-growing shrub, or one with soft stems and a woody base, such as argyranthemums and many pelargoniums.

Succulent Plants with thick fleshy leaves or stems adapted to life under arid conditions. Cacti, with leafless stems swollen with water storage tissue, are examples.

Sucker A shoot which arises from below ground, usually from the roots of a plant.

Synonym An alternative name for a plant. Sometimes a plant has been named by more than one botanist or has been reclassified in the light of further knowledge. In such cases, the oldest or most taxonomically accurate name takes priority.

t **Tap root** The main anchoring root of a plant, particularly applied to trees.

Tender A term to describe any plant vulnerable to frost damage. See also Half-hardy.

Tendril A modified stem or leaf that twines around supports, enabling certain plants, such as sweet peas, grapes, hops and passionflowers, to climb.

Terrestrial Used in reference to plants, such as some bromeliads and orchids which are primarily epiphytic, that have become adapted to living in the soil.

Tessellated A term that describes petals which have a distinct chequered pattern of a contrasting shade or colour – as, for example, Fritillaria meleagris.

Toothed Teeth-like indentations, usually along the margins of leaves, also described as dentate.

Truss A popular term used to describe a cluster of flowers or fruits.

Tuber A thickened fleshy root, as on a dahlia, or an underground stem, such as a potato, which serves as a storage organ, and as a means of surviving periods of cold or drought.

Tufa Soft limestone which, because of its ability to absorb and retain moisture, is often used in rock gardens or troughs, where small alpine plants are able to grow on it.

Tuft Bristly, sometimes mat-like, habit of growth, found particularly in alpine plants.

u **Underplant** To surround and interplant larger plants with smaller ones.

Undulate Leaf, sepal or petal margins that are waved or crimped.

v **Variegated** Leaves – and sometimes petals – that are marked, spotted or otherwise decoratively patterned with a contrasting colour, most commonly cream or gold.

Vegetative Propagation by cuttings, division, layering or grafting, as distinct from propagation with seeds.

w **Weeping** Applied to a tree or shrub of pendulous habit, either natural, as in some species of salix, or artificially induced, as in weeping standard roses.

Page references in *italic* indicate illustrations.

© RD = Reader's Digest Association, MW=Mark Winwood, SC=Sarah Cuttle
All artwork=© Reader's Digest Association

T=Top, B=Bottom, L=Left, R=Right, C=Centre

Cover Rita Ven Den Broek/Photolibrary.com, **1** Gap Photos Ltd/Howard Rice, **2-3** Aaron McCoy/Garden Picture Library, **4** iStockphoto.com/V.J. Matthew, **5** Gap Photos Ltd/Howard Rice, **6** ©RD, **7** TL iStockphoto.com/Lise Gagne, CL CR R ©RD, **8-9** iStockphoto.com, **14** ©RD, **17** TL iStockphoto.com, TR iStockphoto.com/Douglas Freer, **18** © RD/SC, **19-20** © RD/MW, **21** T, BC © RD/SC, BL © RD/MW, **22-24, 25** T © RD/SC. **25** B © RD/MW, **26, 27** TL © RD/SC, **27** TR © RD/MW, **27** B iStockphoto.com/ Peter Eckhardt. **28** © National Soil Resources Institute (NSRI), Cranfield University 2007, **29** BR © RD/MW, **30-36** © RD/MW, **37** © RD/M. Newton, **38** © RD/SC, **39** © RD/MW,**40** iStockphoto.com/James Boulette, **41** © RD/SC. **42** iStockphoto.com, **45** © RD/MW, **46-47** iStockphoto.com, **54** T iStockphoto.com/ Christopher Steer, B iStockphoto.com/Jim Tardio, **56-57** iStockphoto.com/Galina Barskaya, **58-61** © RD. **62-63** © RD/MW, **64** © RD/MW, **65** © RD, **66** iStockphoto.com, **67** T iStockphoto.com/Nicola Stratford, B iStockphoto.com/Melissa Jones, **68** iStockphoto.com/Pattie Steib, **69** R iStockphoto.com/Robert Simon, B iStockphoto.com/Peggy Easterly, **70** iStockphoto.com, **71** T iStockphoto.com/ Paula Stephens, C iStockphoto.com/Melissa Carroll, B iStockphoto.com/Andreas Kaspar, **72, 73** TL iStockphoto.com/Hedda Gjerpen, **73** TR iStockphoto.com/Nancy Nehring, C iStockphoto.com/Tina Lorien, **74** iStockphoto.com/David Hughes, **75** T iStockphoto.com/Christopher Arndt, B iStockphoto.com/John Sigler, **77** iStockphoto.com/Greg Nicholas, **78** iStockphoto.com/Steven Stone, **79, 80** L, CL, CR, R © RD/MW, **80** B © RD/SC, **81** L Photolibrary Group/J. Legate, **81** R, **82-84** © RD/MW, **86** iStockphoto.com, **87** T iStockphoto.com/Mick Smith, B iStockphoto.com/Linda Macpherson, **88** T iStockphoto.com/Ron Hohenhaus, B iStockphoto.com, **89** T iStockphoto.com/Steve McWilliam, B iStockphoto.com/Cheryl A. Meyer, **90** iStockphoto.com/Lise Gagne, **105** iStockphoto.com/Matthew Scherf. **110-116** © RD, **117** TL, TR, BL, BR Garden World Images, **117** CL, C © RD.

Reader's Digest Container Gardening is based on material in *Reader's Digest All Seasons Guide to Gardening*; *Short Cuts to Great Gardens* and *New Encyclopedia of Garden Plants & Flowers* published by The Reader's Digest Association Limited, London

First Edition Copyright © 2007

The Reader's Digest Association Limited, 11 Westferry Circus, Canary Wharf, London E14 4HE **www.readersdigest.co.uk**

Editor Lisa Thomas
Art Editor Austin Taylor
Consultant and writer Daphne Ledward-Hands
Proofreader Barry Gage
Indexer Marie Lorimer

Reader's Digest General Books
Editorial Director Julian Browne
Art Director Anne-Marie Bulat
Managing Editor Alastair Holmes
Head of Book Development Sarah Bloxham
Picture Resource Manager Sarah Stewart-Richardson
Pre-press Account Manager Penelope Grose
Senior Production Controller Deborah Trott
Product Production Manager Claudette Bramble

Origination Colour Systems Limited, London
Printed and bound in China by CT Printing

We are committed to both the quality of our products and the service we provide to our customers. We value your comments, so please feel free to contact us on **08705 113366**, or via our website at **www.readersdigest.co.uk**

If you have any comments about the content of our books, email us at **gbeditorial@readersdigest.co.uk**

ISBN 978 0 276 44261 2
BOOK CODE 400-353-UP000-1
ORACLE CODE 250010674H.00.24